WI GOT STUCK UP TREES
&
Pigeons Fell Down Chimneys

John Brookland

Copyright ©2013 JOHN BROOKLAND

The moral right of the author is hereby asserted in accordance with
The Copyright, Designs and Patents Act 1988
.
All rights reserved.
No part of this publication may be reproduced, stored in a retrieval system, or transmitted, in any form or by any means, without the prior permission in writing of the publisher, nor be otherwise circulated in any form of binding or cover other than that in which it is published and without a similar condition including this condition being imposed on the subsequent purchaser.

ISBN-13: 978-1-479-23041-9
10:1479230413

Available on Kindle
Ebook: ISBN: 978-1-291-00379-6

This is a work of non-fiction and the events it recounts are true,
but some names have been changed.
Any views or comments are purely those of the author.

To Debbie
my soul mate
with thanks for her encouragement,
patience and support.

Also in memory of Louise,
who was kind to all animals and
would have loved this book.

In association with

bitzabooks@gmail.com
facebook.com/bitzabooks

Acknowledgements

Many thanks to Rebecca Mencattelli and Julia Mills, who have read and criticised this book, searching for mistakes and inconsistencies and making comments and suggestions.
Thanks also to Annie Churcher for her expertise and to Chris Reed for searching the RSPCA Archive.

Photo credits:
Photographs on page 122,133,197,210 & 211 by the kind permission of Debbie Jacob.
Other photographs are those of the author.
Images on page 15, 30 & 53 believed to be from London Evening News. Every effort was made to contact copyright holders.

Cover Design/Artwork: 297 Ltd.

Front Cover: Jeremy holds on precariously awaiting rescue. (See page 69).

Table of Contents

Preface 7
The End of an Era 9
The Long Weekend – Saturday 31
Cats in Trouble 60
The Long Weekend – Sunday 88
Swanning About on the River 112
The Night Shift 138
Dogs in Trouble 166
Wildlife Matters 194
People and Places 221
The Final Call 247
Postscript 251

"Since it was inaugurated, the London Night Emergency Service has become an important and essential feature of the Society's work, justifying the boast that the RSPCA is on duty day and night. On a number of occasions members of its staff took great risks to rescue animals under hazardous conditions, climbing derelict buildings, wading through fetid sewers and balancing between electric railway lines".
(RSPCA Annual Report 1960)

Preface

1972: LATE EVENING, LONDON, ENGLAND: a cat is in danger of falling from the top of one of the highest trees in London; a dog is impaled on railings in St. James's Park; a cat is stuck 75 feet up on the roof of Alexandra Palace; a dog is trapped in an escalator at King's Cross Station: who are you going to call?

Well back then, all Londoners, and the other emergency agencies, called upon the services and expertise of the Royal Society for the Prevention of Cruelty to Animals (RSPCA) London Night Emergency Service: a small specialist unit originally based in Piccadilly and set up in 1936 to come to the aid of animals in distress throughout Greater London. It was unique at the time pioneering a night and weekend emergency out of hours veterinary service, alongside a specialist rescue and paramedic unit for animals. It soon became the true fourth emergency service in London with its emergency response vehicle, packed with first aid and rescue equipment, speeding to help injured or trapped animals.

During the 50 years that the Service operated, a small core of dedicated staff worked long hours in basic conditions, often putting themselves at great risk, to rescue, alleviate the suffering and give first aid and treatment to tens of thousands of sick or injured animals in London. This was a time when there were many stray and feral animals roaming the city, when few animal rescue organisations were able or equipped to help and when many Londoners still lived in poverty.

The unit got off to an auspicious start on the night of the 30th. November, 1936, when its staff of two and one van was called out to help rescue animals from the great Crystal Palace fire working alongside 700 Police Officers, 438 Firemen and 88 fire engines. During that first year of operation, they received 334 emergency night calls, which by 1970 had risen, to an amazing 23,759 calls with the ambulance making 1,411 journeys and effecting 161 rescues. The emergency surgery was treating 2,982 animals of worried London pet owners.

This book is an anecdotal account of my experiences when I had the great privilege to work for the unit in the early 1970's. Although the Service helped thousands of animals and pet owners and did incredible work, it is now completely forgotten. Even the RSPCA Archive has only a few vague references. I have written this book so this small piece of London history is not overlooked and that the existence and exploits of this remarkable service are put on record.

1:

The End of an Era

I was leaning against a lamppost in a side street bordering Soho and Covent Garden in Central London. It was eleven o'clock on a cold, drab and dreary night in November and drizzle was beginning to fall. I was gazing up at the roof of the house opposite and attempting to look as inconspicuous as possible. The occasional passer-by would follow my upward gaze and give me a quizzical look, probably suspicious of my motives for loitering. If they had concentrated as hard as I was, they may have noticed the strange sight that had been fascinating me for the last few minutes. Outlined in the shadowy light, they could have caught sight of a cat's hindquarters and tail, waving violently from side to side. Had they waited around a few moments longer, they might even have heard the growls of anger and frustration reverberating from the bottom of the drainpipe opposite.

I had already established that the member of the public, who had called us, was indeed right when she had reported a cat apparently stuck in the drainpipe and guttering of a house. How he managed to get himself into this predicament was another matter. Perhaps the cat was on his nightly prowl on the roof when he spied a mouse. The mouse might have scampered off and shot down the pipe closely followed by the cat, which having made a valiant attempt to follow suit, only succeeded in getting its front legs and head stuck. For the last hour or so, he had remained in this most undignified and uncomfortable position, until a neighbour opposite saw its plight from her bedroom window. As I pondered the best way of rescuing the poor animal, the woman who had first alerted us came out of her house and approached me.

'I believe I know who the cat belongs to,' she informed me 'there is a lady who lives round the corner with a tom cat called Whiskers that is always getting into trouble. I bet it is hers. Shall I go and knock on her door?'

'That would be very helpful', I said pleasantly.

'How are you going to get the cat down?' she inquired.

'That is a very good question,' I replied 'I think the only course of action is to get some assistance.'

It was time for back up and, as I worked alone on the van, the only help available at this time of night was going to be the London Fire Brigade. I radioed my colleague back at our base to make a telephone call to them, which resulted a few minutes later in the reassuring glow of blue flashing lights against the buildings in the distance. The sight and sound of the Fire Brigade always gave me an adrenaline rush and as usual, they turned up in force and in good humour. The Station Officer, resplendent in white hat, jumped from the engine and I walked over to meet him.

'What have you got for us?' he asked with slight trepidation, as they were never quite sure what to expect when we called them out.

After explaining the situation, I pointed in the direction of the cat to confirm my story and the Officer and his men all gazed upward. I got the disturbing impression at this point that they thought I might have been drinking all evening down the West End and was winding them up for a laugh. Soon, though, each fireman spotted the very mobile tail and was convinced. In no time, they had a ladder propped up against the front of the house near to the now angry cat. At this point the owner of the house appeared, roused by all the noise outside. Embarrassingly, I suddenly realised that I hadn't knocked on his door to inform him of what was occurring. He was in a dressing gown and his face dissolved into a shocked expression at the sight of the ladder and the assembled crowd of firemen and onlookers.

'What on earth are you doing to my house? Is it on fire?' he bleated in despair.

I walked quickly to his side and explained what was happening. His expression soon changed to disbelief as he pirouetted around and stared up at his guttering trying to make out the outline of the cat supposedly trapped there.

'You will be careful, won't you?' he exclaimed, calmer now that he knew his house was not on fire. 'Please don't cause any damage'.

It was volunteered to go up first and assess the situation. I climbed the ladder and, as I neared the top, I could hear the cat alternating from a pitiful meow to a frustrated growl. It was a large tabby and white and as he waved his rear end at me, I could easily see that he was most definitely a tom. The growl became more meaningful when he felt me touch his hindquarters. Whilst trying to calm him with soothing noises, I attempted to pull his head from the pipe. This resulted in violent convulsions as he tried to assist in the matter. He also decided to screech at the top of his voice, which made it appear I was hurting him. Looking down at the tableau below me, I could see the upturned faces of the small attentive audience, who always seem to gather at such incidents. The owner of the house was rushing from one fireman to the next with plaintive cries of 'you will be careful? Don't damage my house will you.'

To add to the confusion below, the owner of the cat arrived at this point and proceeded to run from one person to another pleading for information.

'Please help my poor Whiskers,' she cried 'he must be so frightened'.

I made one more gentle effort to pull Whiskers out, but the forequarters of the cat did not intend to join the rest of him in the open air. I returned to ground level, where a discussion ensued while the house owner hopped around the perimeter of us trying to listen to our plans for the likely destruction of his house.

'It's no good', I said, 'I can't budge the cat'.

The firemen took turns going up to see the problem for themselves. They also tried gentle persuasion as I had done, but to no avail and there was general agreement that drastic action was required. The Station Officer suggested that we should get the whole situation down to ground level so that we could get to grips with the problem. The poor householder was visibly going pale as it dawned on him what they planned to do.

'I forbid you to do any damage to my property. You will all pay you know.' he warned.

'Don't worry sir I'm sure the RSPCA will see you all right for any damage we cause', he smiled giving me a sly wink.

He was obviously not convinced and watched in horror as another ladder was placed against the front of his house and two firemen climbed up armed with a crowbar and a hammer. On arriving level with Whiskers' hindquarters, the two proceeded to wrench the pipe off the wall. While one held onto it, his colleague pulled the guttering away and supported the now very angry feline. The men descended in tandem preceded by a shower of debris, clutching the pipe and the backside of poor Whiskers. The house owner was now apoplectic. We stood in a circle contemplating the six foot section containing the flailing tail and hind legs.

'We're not going to see a thing out here in the dark', stated a fireman.

'You can come round to my house. It's only a few yards away', offered Whiskers owner.

The offer was accepted and we all trooped off leaving the bemused owner of the house staring up at his missing guttering with a dazed expression on his face. Six firemen, the length of pipe containing Whiskers and myself squeezed into a tiny kitchen. We laid it on the kitchen table and stared at it. This was no cheap metalwork, but the original made of cast iron.

'So far so good' said the Station Officer.

'Now what do we do?' asked a fireman.

'How about putting soap round his neck?' suggested another.

'Good idea'.

Washing up liquid was produced and squirted between the cat's body and the pipe and we tried again. Whiskers would not budge.

'This is silly', said a fireman 'We can't do much with six feet of cast iron getting in the way. We'll have to cut it near the cat's head and then we can have a go from both ends'.

The Station Officer turned to me: 'I agree. We have a small workshop at our base. With your permission I suggest we return there and have a go at cutting it'.

We all climbed into the rear cab of the fire engine and drove the short distance to the Fire Station with the pipe across our laps. We retreated to the workshop where it was positioned in a vice and a fireman appeared with a heavy duty hacksaw. The laborious job of sawing through the thick cast iron began. I held and stroked the rear end of Whiskers to try to keep him calm. It took quite a long time and everyone had to take a turn, as it was hot work. Amazingly, Whiskers was very still throughout the operation and I had to keep checking to make sure he was OK. Eventually we ended up with a foot long piece and everyone took turns to look into it to see the startled face of Whiskers. His scared eyes stared pitifully out at us and he made frantic attempts to free himself now that he could see light. After considerable discussion and a multitude of suggestions, it was decided to try to saw through lengthways and prise it apart. This was going to be a very delicate job so the first priority was a tray of steaming cups of tea to give everyone the strength and fortitude for the task ahead.

Whiskers had to endure a further 40 minutes of stress as the sawing continued. This had to be done with great care so as not to injure him or shower him with sharp filings. Throughout all this activity, the stoic Whiskers was getting hot and agitated, so at every opportunity we gave him time to rest and calm down. We were also getting very hot and bothered by the time the pipe was finally sawn through. It was then a question of prising it open slightly. This again was carefully done and suddenly after three hours of work, the head and front legs of Whiskers popped out into the open.

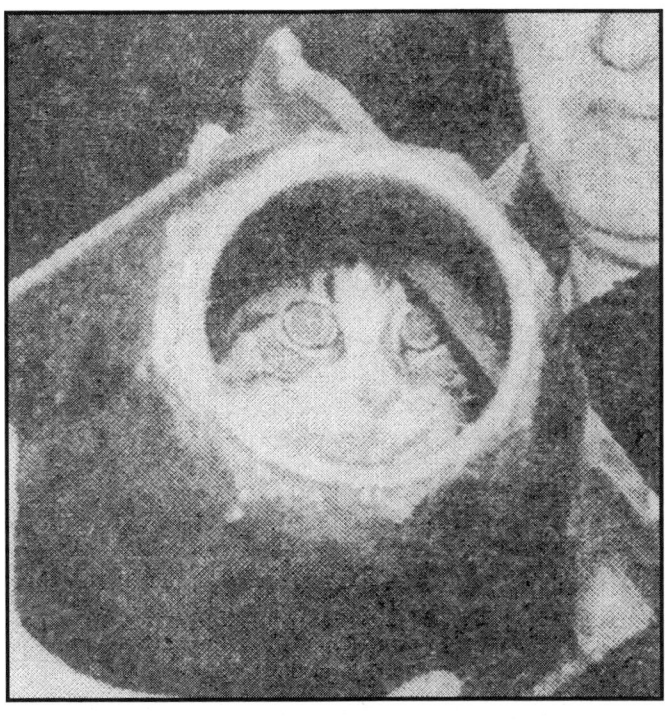

Whiskers soon after his release from the pipe.

There were cheers all round as he came free and a lot of self-congratulation. I placed Whiskers on the floor where he worryingly panted for breath for a while before shaking himself. He then scratched his neck a few times and sat nonchalantly licking his paws as though embarrassed. The owner was overjoyed and scooped him up for a cuddle. A quick examination showed that the only injury he had suffered was a graze on his neck. The owner was given the offending top of the drainpipe as a souvenir. Another round of tea appeared from nowhere and the obligatory saucer of milk was placed in front of Whiskers. Then everyone sat around excitedly talking about the night's events. Looking round the faces of the assembled firemen, who must have been a hardened lot with the terrible incidents and sights they had to deal with on a daily basis, it was wonderful to see that they appeared to get so much satisfaction out of rescuing helpless animals.

Three and a half hours after first sighting the plight of Whiskers, I finally left Soho Fire Station and flopped into my van. It was now nearly three o'clock in the morning and time to return to my base in North London. Being ten hours into my fifteen-hour shift, I was exhausted and exhilarated all at the same time. As I carefully drove through the deserted London streets, I just couldn't believe how lucky I was. I had wanted to find a job where I could physically help save animals lives and feel that I was really doing something to make a difference and I had found it by working for the RSPCA London Night Emergency Service.

It was a dream job to work nightly alongside the other emergency services coming to the aid of trapped or seriously injured animals involved in accidents with cars and trains, fires, explosions and bizarre rescues.

It was 1972 and I had been working for the Night Emergency Service, known to RSPCA staff as 'NES', for just a few months. It had been operating from a basement unit at the Society's headquarters in the West End of London and had been kept very busy since 1936 as it was a time before the proliferation of small animal charities and specialist wildlife rescue organisations. There were no local council dog wardens or animal welfare officers and the Police took little interest in anything involving an animal. It was a time before the

London Fire Brigade operated its own animal rescue teams and had specialised equipment. Many private vets only operated a haphazard after hour's service. It was a London where latch key dogs roamed the streets in their hundreds, where stray and feral cats lived and bred on the old bombsites which had still not been redeveloped nearly three decades after the war and when large numbers of Londoners still lived in poverty. The Metropolitan and Transport Police, River Police, London Fire Brigade and Ambulance Service, Social Services, London Underground, British Rail, Royal Parks, Local Authorities and especially the London public all turned to the NES at night and weekends for advice and assistance. It was the only organisation that operated an out of hour's rapid response vehicle to carry out specialised rescues and collect injured or sick animals.

At 5.30 pm, as all the RSPCA Headquarters staff headed homeward, this tiny unit took over the reins of the world's largest animal welfare organisation. All the offices and corridors became dark and silent and the telephones were transferred to an office in the basement. Every weekday night and throughout the weekend, this small unit *was* the RSPCA, not just for the citizens of London, but for many others as well. The staff worked extremely long hours in basic conditions, which would be illegal today. The weekend shift alone lasted from midday on the Saturday through to Monday morning, a total of 44 hours. Luckily, it was possible for the staff of three to sleep when the calls upon their services diminished in the early hours. During each shift or part of the shift, the three members of the team took turns to either answer the telephone, drive the ambulance or to be the nurse and attend to the sick or injured animals that were hurried in by worried owners. The least popular duty with many was answering the telephone as this could be stressful, but the most anticipated option was driving and attending unusual incidents.

I had come to London in 1970 and had started work for the RSPCA in their veterinary clinic next door to the Angel Islington Underground Station. It was at this clinic while training to be an animal nurse that I came across these eccentric uniformed RSPCA men wearing 'Emergency Service' shoulder flashes who popped in occasionally first thing in the morning on their way back to their base after a call out. Over a cup of tea, they animatedly related tales of animal rescues they had performed during the night. I was immediately envious of them as their job appeared far more exciting than my mundane job of restraining animals for the vet and mopping floors at the clinic.

I immediately decided that I wanted to work with them, but I was soon to discover that it was very difficult to get a place on the NES as there were only six officers and you required a lot of experience in animal care to stand any chance. At that time, the RSPCA had a network of veterinary clinics spread all over London. Many of these had an animal ambulance operating from them to collect injured and trapped stray animals. Luckily, for me, a few months after starting work at the clinic, the animal ambulance job became available and I immediately applied and was successful. I could hardly contain my excitement, as my area was the whole of the East End and the City of London, an interesting part of London to work in. On my first day as driver, I had jumped eagerly into my van armed with a copy of the London A-Z and a first aid box whilst trying to master the two-way radio. However, my elation was short lived when I realised that having only passed my driving test six months earlier, and apart from driving my father's car along quiet country roads in deepest Kent, I had no experience of negotiating the busy London streets. I didn't have a clue where I was going; Google maps and sat navs were still the stuff of science fiction.

I received no training as an animal ambulance driver and it was a case of on the job learning. I didn't have a uniform, just a plain white coat that made me look like a butcher. I did receive a second-hand uniform after a few weeks, but unfortunately, this was several sizes too big. The trouser bottoms dragged along the ground and I couldn't find my hands in the sleeves, but I felt very official. I only had two accidents in the first month, something I was proud of; my Manager did not share this pride, especially as one accident involved ramming a human ambulance: very embarrassing! In the beginning, it was a nightmare, as after navigating a few streets, I had to pull over and check my map book. I spent many happy hours driving in circles round one-way systems and heading in the wrong direction. Eventually though I got to know my area really well and could speed along to emergencies such as road accidents involving dogs, in impressive time. If I couldn't get on the NES then this was the second best option as I was out all day driving round my area of London getting involved in rescues and collecting injured animals. It was a wonderful way of gaining experience.

Having moved to London at eighteen from the countryside in order to work, I often felt lonely in the evenings during the early months and I was relatively naive of city life having only visited London three times before. Having become friendly with some of the NES staff, it seemed a good idea to go and visit them on boring evenings or weekends. In fact their office had become a hangout for many staff, who had perhaps been on a night out in the West End or, like me, wanted company through a dull evening at home. It was a good thing to befriend them and become welcome rather than tolerated, as there was also the chance of covering a shift during staff holidays or sickness. As a very young newcomer to the Society, I was in awe of these guys and did my best to "keep in" with them.

Therefore, I would leave my soulless accommodation in Swiss Cottage, jump on the Underground and arrive at the bright lights and frenzied activity of Piccadilly Circus. I then headed for Jermyn Street just a few hundred yards away and passed by the entrance of the RSPCA National Headquarters, which had been at number 105 since 1869. It was a huge building on several floors, with a great old staircase and a rickety Victorian lift. During the working day, a concierge resplendent in uniform and peaked cap stood on the steps at the front entrance to usher visitors in. The building smelled of ancient wood, dust and age and was crammed with offices. There was a maze of staircases and corridors winding their way through it. When the staff cheerfully vacated their offices in the evening, the building became hushed and dark as the huge front doors were closed and locked. From the front, it looked as though the mighty RSPCA was dormant for the night, but the building was never completely closed.

I continued along Jermyn Street and turned left into Duke of York Street, where a typical West End pub, the

Red Lion, stood on the right. Opposite the pub was a wide alley and anyone would be hard pressed to see the street sign in the dark, but this dingy, uninviting cul-de-sac was named Apple Tree Yard. It was not a name to conjure up any particular memories or events and it was not listed in any guidebook. If you look today, you will find it has changed completely with the original buildings on both sides demolished. I walked half way down and on the left-hand side; there was a nondescript door with a dull light above it. This was the back entrance to 105 Jermyn Street. Although there was no large neon sign, every member of the public, London cabbie and the Police knew that at night, if they had an animal in distress or in need of rescuing, this was the place to contact or come to. Visitors had a hint they were in the right place as an ambulance with RSPCA Emergency Service markings was usually parked by the door. It was crammed with useful equipment to help rescue any animal in difficulties.

I walked down three steps and along a short, badly lit corridor deep in the basement. At the end, I turned right through into a shabby waiting room, lined with plastic chairs and smelling strongly of disinfectant. There was no reception desk here, but if I peered to the left, I could see the open door of an examination room, where the staff checked any animal brought into them. These were the days before modern drugs and high tech veterinary machines, so there was just basic equipment to attend to animals that had been hit by cars or trains or had suddenly fallen seriously ill. Behind this room was a small recovery area with cages for the animals to get over the shock of whatever trauma they had suffered.

If you rang the bell on the wall a door on the right would open and an often dishevelled, strangely dressed and bleary-eyed man would welcome you. The time of night and which part of the 55-hour shift you had caught him on dictated how dishevelled, bleary eyed and welcoming he was. I poked my head round the door and hoped to be granted entry. I was now in the realms of the RSPCA Night Emergency Service.

The inner sanctum was a large room some twenty feet square. Being mainly beneath ground level there was little natural light and the room had a dingy but restful feel by day or night. In fact, it was often difficult to know whether it was day or night until you went outside. On one wall was a large map of Greater London where an address could be pinpointed. Along another wall were six staff lockers and in a corner a kitchenette with the sink piled high with an assortment of cracked and grubby mugs, which provided the much-needed caffeine. Scattered around the room were an array of easy chairs in various states of dilapidation and comfort. In a further corner there was a bunk bed, beside it a large desk with three telephones. This was the most important part of the room and the person answering these emergency lines had the responsibility, through their guile, knowledge and inventiveness, for the health and welfare of hundreds of animals in the city. Each night they would ring constantly until the early hours. NES was intended mainly to help sick, injured or trapped stray animals in distress and provide emergency treatment and advice to owners of animals who could not afford private veterinary surgeons. The telephonist for the shift handed out advice, suggested first aid, recommended whether animals should be brought in for treatment or arranged for the ambulance to attend.

I greeted whoever was sitting at the desk or lounging in the chairs and then always tried to sit near the telephones. Harry and Nick were two of the doyens when it came to answering them. Harry had been on the Society for some 35 years and had an amazing deep authoritative voice. He had a habit of calling everyone 'my dear': 'Sounds very much like an abscess to me, my dear. Bathe it with warm salt water and keep the wound open. Get it along to your vet in the morning my dear. It will be alright'.

Nick was also a font of knowledge on animals and he later did great work with international animal organisations. He appeared to live on strong tea and toast, which he didn't touch unless it was cremated. He would tip an old electric fire on its back and lay slices of bread over the grill, watching and turning them while he gave advice. I sat and listened to Harry and Nick reassuring worried owners and tried to absorb all the information they gave for future reference. I gained so much knowledge just sitting and listening to them. I was both entranced and puzzled at their advice which often sounded like a witches brew. There was mention of Friars Balsam, Fullers Earth, China Clay, Bicarbonate of Soda and Epsom Salts to name a few. Such items were what pet owners at the time, might have in their cupboards, which they could use for emergency first aid on their pet.

I sat in this cosy little world, making the odd cup of tea and hoping that I might be able to do something to help. Sometimes it was just a case of going out and helping to get a take away meal. On a couple of occasions I was asked to nip up to the only 24-hour chemist in London at the time at Boots in Piccadilly Circus. It was only to fill a prescription for drugs the duty vet was in urgent need of, but I felt I was doing something important. It was fun to quickly walk through the busy West End streets, thronged with people enjoying a night out. There was also that slight chance that something exciting might happen and I might be asked whether I fancied going out on the ambulance to help. It was always a double-edged scenario as although I wanted to go on a rescue, it might involve the pain and suffering of an animal and this was obviously something I didn't want to happen:

* * *

I could make out blue flashing lights ahead reflecting off the trees and buildings. Ray the driver at NES that night had just made a manic drive through the busy streets screeching round St. James's Square, almost on two wheels and slamming me into the passenger door on our way to St. James's Park. All NES drivers were slightly mad and Ray was no exception. Driving the ambulance at high speed on journeys all over Greater London in response to emergency calls from the Police, Fire Brigade or members of the public was the most popular facet of the job. This was particularly so late at night or in the early hours, when the empty streets of that time allowed quick dashes from one side of London to the other. These were of course in the days before speed cameras and when London's streets were almost deserted after midnight.

NES had just received a telephone call reporting a dog impaled on railings and I had been given the nod that I could go and help. Being so close to the base we had made it to the park in good time, but the London

Fire Brigade had arrived before us. As we pulled up beside the fire tender I could see a small group of people and firemen over by the park railings. A fireman spotted us and met us half way.

'I am so glad to see you. Thanks for getting here so quickly', he said. 'A dog has tried to jump the park railings and didn't make it. He is impaled right on top. I'm afraid there are a few hysterical people present giving us some grief, but we did not want to remove the dog until you arrived. We couldn't get hold of a vet'.

We arrived at the tightly knit group of concerned bystanders.

'Out of the way please,' said the fireman, 'The RSPCA is here now so give us some room.'

Two firemen, along with another man, were standing either side of the railings holding and supporting a load under a blanket.

'We have been supporting the dog's weight since we arrived, but he screams in pain if we try and move him', explained one.

'Yeh, we didn't want to lift him off without someone like you here in case the spike causes a lot of damage and he bleeds to death.'

In these situations, when the likelihood of something going seriously wrong was more than likely, the onus was usually put completely on the shoulders of the RSPCA officers present. We were not vets and we couldn't give treatment to save the dog if something did go wrong, but as always, the RSPCA Emergency Service were the only organisation available.

'Let's take a look,' Ray said.

The blanket was removed and the dog instinctively flinched, cried out in pain and panicked causing a woman behind me to join in the cries. When a powerful torch lit up the scene, it resulted in more struggling. The firemen had to hang on tightly to stop the dog hurting himself further. We crouched underneath and, with the aid of the torch beam could see that the iron-railing spike had entered through the armpit, which although painful and terrible, was better than through the stomach or chest as often happened. The dog was relatively thin and so his weight hadn't torn too big a hole in his flesh. There was a little blood, but on checking the gums and eyes, he did not appear too shocked.

'Well I think we should try and lift him off. John, can you nip back to the van and get the first aid box', instructed Ray.

When I returned, Ray asked me to get a bandage out and tie it round the dog's nose. This had a double purpose: one to stop any attempts at biting and the other to muffle any screams caused by the pain. With the bandage on I helped take the dog's weight while Ray positioned himself underneath.

'Let's give it a go. I'll stay under here and you lift when I say. I'll try and guide the dog off the spike.' Ray informed us.

We all steadied ourselves and then Ray shouted 'one, two, and three, LIFT!'

The dog came off the spike like a knife out of butter and Ray took another quick look at the wound while I held him. Luckily, there was no spurting blood so he wasn't going to bleed to death. I carried him to the ambulance where I settled him in the back under a blanket. I uttered a few soothing words and gave him a stroke and amazingly he didn't appear to be that concerned; only relieved to be released from his predicament. There were thanks and congratulations all round: another NES rescue had been successful and I had been part of it. We returned more slowly this time back to Apple Tree Yard. I carried the dog into the small surgery where Nick gave him a closer examination, telephoned the duty vet and gave some medication. Next morning he was transported to the RSPCA hospital in Putney where his wound was sutured and a relieved and thankful owner claimed him.

*   *   *

NES was staffed by an eclectic mix of individuals who had vast experience with all kinds of animals and the injuries and the predicaments they got into. Some of them had worked for the Society a long time and others came and went. One exuberant member was Vic, who with his huge long beard that virtually covered his face, was a David Bellamy character. He was mad on reptiles and sometimes had one or two secreted on his person, which he was keen to show off to you. He was often chef for the shift and wasn't averse to cooking up some strange meals:

'Tastes great Vic - what is it?'

'Tinned dog food with loads of curry powder: supplies are a bit short.'

Paul, who was also a little madcap, carried out extraordinary animal rescues at immense risk to himself often swinging from ropes at great height and scaling derelict buildings. Tony was another bearded member of staff who arrived from New Zealand to study the work of the RSPCA and stayed to work for them.

The RSPCA did not employ many of its own vets and private vets from Central London operated most of the emergency clinics. Many of these in the late sixties and early seventies were characters and celebrities in their own right. This often resulted in strange goings on. There was one, who was often inebriated on arrival and he would be propped in a chair in the night room with a coffee while the night staff attended to the animals. He was told the following morning which animals he had seen and what treatment he had given.

The building at night was an eerie and frightening place. One duty the staff undertook was to wander the maze of corridors and offices over the six floors to check that all lights were off and all was safe. The building smelt very old and reeked of polished wood and dust with background creaks and groans after a hundred years of use. In the middle there was a ground to rooftop well, allowing light to penetrate into the centre of the old building. This was traversed by an iron bridge with a drop to the basement. There was a story that an RSPCA Inspector had committed suicide on this bridge by shooting himself with a humane pistol designed to shoot horses. It was believed that his ghost still stalked the bridge and corridors. On some occasions when there was a large group of staff gathered, such games as hide and seek were instigated which involved roaming the dozens of darkened corridors and offices. This could be a very spooky and frightening experience, particularly when you traversed the iron bridge. All these tales and antics, often exaggerated, gave the Night Staff an almost mythical status and most young male members of staff dreamed of joining their ranks, but vacancies were rare. I was one of these hopefuls and I spent a lot of time enjoying the atmosphere and getting "in" with the Night Staff.

The Society decided to move from Jermyn Street to larger and brighter offices in the countryside of West Sussex, so after 103 years of service the headquarters was to close. Staff and public were shocked at the announcement, as it seemed inconceivable that this wonderful building, which had seen so much history, could be demolished. With the headquarters closing, the fate of the NES and its 36 years of dedicated service was in the balance. There was considerable public outcry and representations were made to try to keep it operating from the basement or somewhere nearby, but to no avail. Eventually it was decided to resurrect the service in a slightly different guise, by dividing it between two hospitals that the RSPCA operated in London. One was situated in Putney and would cover the Western part of London while the other hospital in Finsbury Park would cover the East, the City and West End. As the Emergency Service had been located in the West End for so long, there was a problem about informing the public of its move. Notices were placed in the London evening newspapers to inform everyone that Apple Tree Yard was no longer going to be the home of NES. Such had been the impact of the NES on Londoners that for months afterwards pet owners still arrived unannounced at the back door of Jermyn Street, clutching their sick or injured pets. A member of staff led a lonely and solitary existence there for three months redirecting people to the hospitals.

Everyone was both saddened and disappointed that this era had ended, but there was nothing that could be done. It was progress. Several of the staff decided not to make the move, as it just wouldn't be the same for them. This left opportunities for those of us who were yearning to join the Night Staff. So in 1972, I immediately applied and was accepted and I started on the new Night Emergency Service at Finsbury Park. I had not succeeded in my ambition of working with many of the old staff in the atmospheric and lively

Jermyn Street basement in the West End, but it was great to be in at the beginning of a new era.

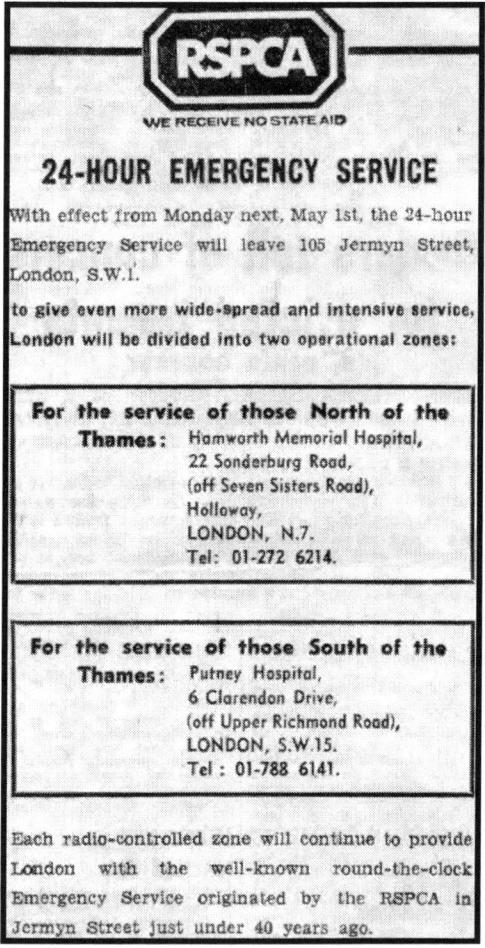

Such had been the impact of the Night Service on Londoners, that for months after it closed people continued to turn up at the back door of Jermyn Street with their sick or injured pets

2:

The Long Weekend - Saturday

'You're hurting him. Leave him alone', cried the young woman as she grabbed at my arm.

I gave her the best stony stare I could muster and continued attempting to get a bandage round the nose of her very large, male, Great Dane. She gave me such a glare that I thought she was going to physically assault me, but her boyfriend pulled her back. Fifteen minutes earlier, we had received a call to attend King's Cross Underground Station, as our assistance was required urgently, with a dog trapped in an escalator. This was a typical and regular weekend call out, particularly on hot summer weekends. We treated these incidents as real emergencies as they usually involved great pain and injury to the dogs. I had made record time hurtling down the long straight Caledonian Road parking illegally outside the Station. Terry, a colleague had accompanied me, as it often proved a difficult rescue. He had grabbed a first aid kit and followed me. At the top of one of the escalators, we came across a group of Underground staff. They parted on our approach and we could see a sobbing young woman crouched over a massive Great Dane, which was loudly whimpering every minute or so, and with each scream the owner was becoming more hysterical. How anyone in their right mind could consider taking such a large and unco-ordinated dog onto an escalator was beyond my comprehension and made me very angry.

During the summer, if it was a nice day, owners would take their dogs with them to London parks and they would make the trip on the Underground. They often failed to realise that it is a legal requirement to carry them in your arms or, alternatively and preferably, to use the stairs. Dogs like to feel a stable surface beneath them and do not like or understand movement under their paws. They are also unaware that at the end they are supposed to jump from the moving ground beneath them to solid ground. Even if they did, large dogs do not have the co-ordination to accomplish this successfully.

Many Stations still had the pre-war wooden escalators that had high ridged wooden slats on the steps. These left a large gap as they disappeared under the metal plate. Dogs riding them were often unable to launch all four legs off the moving steps simultaneously when they reached the end and this resulted in one or more paws or toenails being caught and shredded under the metal plate until someone pressed the emergency stop button. The dog would be in agony and traumatised by the event. All these wooden ones have mercifully been replaced so the problem has disappeared.

In this case, the toes of both front paws were trapped. I finally got the bandage over the dog's nose and, with the help of Terry, tied it round the back of its neck. He began to twist and turn, which caused him more pain and he began to squeal. The owner started to scream at me again and we were all getting very stressed.

'You've tied it too tight,' she wailed and threw herself over the dog.

'For heaven's sake please let us help your dog and give us a bit of room,' shouted Terry.

'What is the dog's name?' I asked

'King,' she wailed.

'Well the sooner you get out of the way the quicker we can help King.'

'I can't leave my baby.'

At this point, we decided to call upon the services of a Transport Policeman, who was hovering behind us. He had to almost forcibly pull the owner out of the way. Once she had moved, Terry and I got down to business. I knelt down and took a close look at the paws and I immediately saw that the claws and some of the toes were well under the metal plate. I tentatively tried to pull one of the paws, while Terry held on, but it wouldn't budge and the dog screamed again producing another torrent of abuse from the restrained owner.

'Are the engineers on their way?' I asked the Station Foreman who was kneeling beside us.

'Yep, but they will be another five minutes or so yet,' he advised.

'How can you let my poor baby suffer for that long? Do something,' shouted the woman.

'Well you should have thought of your poor baby before taking him on here. Didn't you see the big signs plastered at the bottom, telling you to use the stairs with dogs? They are there for this sole reason.' We were beginning to get a little irritated with her.

'Quite right,' continued the Station Foreman, 'We will be taking your details as soon as we have the dog free, as you have committed an offence and will be fined for this.'

'We will have to sedate him,' Terry said.

In our first aid box, we carried a sedative. Terry filled a syringe and I gave King the injection.

'We have given him something to make him relax and a little sleepy,' I explained.

I put a blanket over King and allowed her to comfort him until the engineers arrived and then I ushered her out of the way again. The engineers quickly removed the bolts.

'Lift the plate slowly if you can, so that he doesn't panic with any pain,' I asked.

King was pretty relaxed now and only made a low whimper when the plate was raised; after being trapped for thirty minutes he was finally free. This was a cue for lots of sobbing and cuddles from his owner. Surprisingly, the paws had suffered only superficial damage: a couple of torn claws and some cuts on the toes. I wanted to take him back to the hospital for treatment, but the owner wouldn't hear of it. Probably suspicious of our intentions and not wanting to get involved with us she made to walk away, but was detained by the Police. I could not make her hand over the dog and could only advise that she took him to a vet herself. We didn't get a word of thanks, which wasn't unusual in these circumstances. We packed up our gear and headed back to the van. As we reached it, I could hear our base calling over the radio and Terry grabbed the mike.

'Go ahead base,' he answered.

'I was wondering what had happened to you' said our colleague, Ray. This was long before the advent of the mobile telephone, so often we were out of contact for a long time.

'It got a bit involved.'

'Sorry, but believe it or not, I have got another dog in an escalator at Liverpool Street Circle Line,' he informed us.

It was unusual to get two such calls at the same time. Luckily it was a straight run and not too far away. We would have to go through the whole procedure again. It was going to be a busy weekend.

*   *   *

Moving the Night Emergency Service to its new bases was achieved with few problems. Initially we had to sleep on camp beds in the hospital reception while our night room was sorted out, but eventually we received the huge old bunk beds from Jermyn Street, which was a reminder at least of the old Night Service. For the first few months I was teamed up with one of the old Jermyn Street guys who had decided to make the move. It was the deep voiced Harry of the "my dears". Harry did not like driving as he felt he was too old and had been there and done it all before. This was brilliant for me as it allowed me to get out and about on all the rescues. I could not wait to start my first shift and just the thought of working nights was thrilling and new to me. My first shift was the daunting 44 hour marathon beginning at midday on Saturday and finishing at eight o'clock on the Monday morning. There were no official breaks, but we grabbed meals during quiet periods. We obtained food for the weekend from the local supermarket on our way in. We had a small kitchen to cook meals in, but usually by Sunday evening, we were both too tired to cook so resorted to takeaways. If I only managed a few hours' sleep on the Saturday night, then my energy and enthusiasm was often wearing a bit thin by late on Sunday night. You had to get on well with your colleague as you spent a lot of time together. It was a punishing shift, but we enjoyed it and we lived in our own little world during that time.

This little world was the RSPCA Sir Harold Harmsworth Veterinary Hospital in North London just off the Seven Sisters Road at Finsbury Park. At the time it was probably the largest, most modern and best-equipped veterinary hospital in the country. It was a truly impressive place, but in 1973 when the Headquarters in Jermyn Street closed down, the relatively quiet existence at the hospital was shattered. The RSPCA was reorganized in London and many of the clinics closed; the hospital became the administrative centre and main clinic for London north of the Thames. It was nearly twenty years later that it became famous through the BBC TV series "Animal Hospital" with Rolf Harris. Five vets and twenty staff looked after over one hundred inpatients in eight wards and treated the same amount of outpatients daily during the week. But as with the old Night Service, in the evenings and at weekends two emergency staff and one nurse manned the building.

It was an eventful time to be living and working in London. Edward Heath was Prime Minister and there was a lot of unrest with TUC strikes over pay and CND marches: we never quite knew what was going on. At one point electricity was rationed and we were reduced to examining the animals by gas lamps and spent hours huddled over gas fires. There was the 3 day week, although this didn't affect our fifty-five hour week, and then petrol was rationed. Garages couldn't pump it out of the underground tanks and everyone was feverishly driving around looking for fuel. Long queues gathered outside garages causing traffic chaos. Luckily, we managed to get a local garage to give us priority and fill our ambulances out of sight and without waiting. Street lights were switched off, even all the famous lights in Piccadilly Circus. We had the IRA bombings of King's Cross Station and other places, which made you nervous of being in London. Next we had a refuse strike and streets were rendered impassable to traffic by huge mountains of rubbish bags; not that the stray dogs and cats minded or the rats - they had a field day. Finally, the Dockers also decided to strike. From my little transistor radio hanging from the rear view mirror of the van, I was listening to the likes of David Bowie, Led Zeppelin and Bob Marley. At the cinema, the Godfather, Clockwork Orange, Dirty Harry and The French Connection were showing. On television it was Monty Python, Steptoe and Son and Columbo. Carnaby Street and Soho were still thriving. Locally we had the Arsenal football ground on our doorstep and on match days, it was a nightmare to get out in the ambulance on a Saturday afternoon. Then in the evening, we had the hazard of the old Astoria, which had been reinvented as the Rainbow venue, which became extremely popular. Through all this life went on.

* * *

The German Hospital, situated in an area called Homerton, in the East End of London, telephoned one Saturday to say that a lady had been admitted and was likely to remain in for a while. She owned several budgerigars that were left in her flat and required looking after. The nurse said that they could not contact a Social Worker, as it was a weekend, so could we assist with the birds. I asked if I could collect her house keys from the hospital. I was informed that the old lady was reluctant to relinquish either her keys or any other personal possessions to them and they hoped I could persuade her.

I drove there and parked outside the austere buildings. The hospital had an incredible history. It was built in 1845 to provide treatment for the huge German immigrant population that lived in poverty in the East End. Being unable to speak English and too poor to get treatment elsewhere, the hospital was built by a German institution and staffed entirely by German doctors and nurses to cater for them. Florence Nightingale was apparently inspired by the work done there. During the Second World War, the staff were interned, and the hospital became part of the NHS and was used mainly for elderly people with mental health issues. It closed in 1987. I was met by the ward sister, who led me along the row of beds. She eventually stopped at the foot of one containing a stocky lady, who was sitting upright in the bed clutching her handbag and muttering to herself.

'This is Ruby,' the Sister announced.

Ruby looked as though she had led a rough life, which obviously hadn't helped her temperament and she just glared at us.

'Ruby, this nice man from the RSPCA is going to look after your birds while you are with us,' the Sister said sweetly.

'Oh is he. Go away; I'm not talking to you,' she shouted.

'Now come on Ruby, you cannot leave the poor birds without care. You don't want them to come to any harm, do you? Someone has got to feed them?' the Sister pleaded.

'Birds ul be orright.' muttered Ruby, 'You got no right to meddle. I'll be 'owt o 'ere soon. Don't you worry.'

'I'm afraid you'll be in here quite some time,' persevered the Sister.

'Aw shut up. You don't nah nuthin. Them bird's ul be orright I tell you.'

We spent some twenty minutes attempting to persuade Ruby to let me help, but to no avail. She just sat clutching her bag and refusing to hand over her keys. I decided to go round to her house to take a look. It was a terraced house converted into two apartments and Ruby lived on the ground floor. The neighbour upstairs allowed me into the hallway and showed me two doors. Both doors had heavy padlocks on them and, from all accounts, the neighbours were not in Ruby's good books and so were not on speaking terms. For this reason they did not have spare keys and I could not break in. I tried looking through the dirty windows, but could not catch sight of the birds. I decided to call into the local police station on the off chance that they might be able to help. I chatted to the Desk Sergeant and discovered that he knew Ruby quite well as she was a local character and often called in for a chat and company. He was not at all surprised to hear that she was not co-operative. He offered to come to the hospital with me as it was a quiet afternoon and he wanted the chance to get out for a while. When we arrived at Ruby's bedside we noticed she had put her handbag on the bedside chair. She also appeared to brighten at the sight of her friend the Sergeant.

'Hello Ruby. What have you been up to then old girl?' He then proceeded to chat aimlessly with her for a few minutes, eventually bringing the conversation back round to the budgerigars. Directly he mentioned them, she became suspicious and was back to her defensive self.

'You leave them birds alone I tell you. They my birds and I don won anyone messin' with 'em.'

The Sister tried to intervene again. and was immediately told to "shut up" and we were back where we started. The Sergeant though had an idea, and out of the earshot of Ruby, explained it to us. The master plan was for him to keep her occupied while the Sister unobtrusively drew the curtains round her bed and across the bedside table and chair. I was then to remove the keys from her bag, which would be hidden by the curtain. It seemed a good idea and it worked to perfection with Ruby totally unaware that her keys had gone. I did not usually stoop to such measures and steal old ladies' keys, but it was the only way we could attend to her budgerigars. I said goodbye to Ruby telling her she had won and we left her with a satisfied smirk on her face.

I returned to her flat with the Sergeant and we unlocked the large padlocks. The flat was in quite a state and smelt of damp, grease and stale food. Amongst all the old and faded furniture, we found two Victorian looking cages containing four budgerigars. They were in quite a messy state and needed a good clean. We carried the cages to my van with the frightened birds flapping about wildly and drove back via the hospital to return the keys. Ruby had not noticed they had disappeared and the Sister said she would put them back into her bag. The hospital promised to let us know well in advance of her discharge so that I could return the birds in a similar fashion to how I had acquired them. In that way Ruby would be completely innocent of what had occurred. I could see this backfiring on me, but agreed.

As it turned out I was right. Ruby decided to discharge herself two days later against hospital advice. We were not informed straight away, so Ruby returned home, found her birds missing and went down to the Police Station to report them stolen. Luckily the same Sergeant was on duty and managed to explain and pacify her. I eventually turned up with the budgerigars expecting to be greeted with a torrent of abuse, but she was so pleased to see her beloved birds back, that she actually welcomed me. As I left, she shouted after me, "I told you me birds al be orright!"

*   *   *

At the beginning of each shift, the first duty of the driver was to check the emergency response van and its equipment. When I was initially a driver, the RSPCA used large cumbersome Austin vans, which had the gear lever on the steering column. They were not particularly easy or fun to drive in London traffic, but we were then given Ford Escort vans which were a dream to drive. The van was equipped with baskets, an assortment of dog leads and collars, blankets, nets, torches, rope ladder, swan hook, drain rods, ropes, screwdrivers, hammers, saws and many other tools and items useful for catching, holding or rescuing animals. It even had an animal stretcher.

The most important and useful piece of equipment was the dog grasper: a hollow metal pole with a rope noose at the end. It looks a cruel implement, but if used correctly, it was a godsend for handling many types of unfriendly animals. It has been in use since the First World War, when an RSPCA Inspector invented it in 1917. He came up with the idea whilst rescuing animals from beneath debris, following a Zeppelin bombing raid on Silvertown in the London Dock area. The idea is to place the noose over the head of a dog or cat and then tighten the noose by pulling the rope, which is threaded through the hollow pole.

I had to be ready for any eventuality, as I never knew what incident I might get involved in. I carried a first aid box with bandages, tape, scissors, forceps, syringes, needles, antiseptics and an injectable sedative plus a drug we used for euthanasia. The van was connected to the hospital by a two way radio.

* * *

I was at a house just off the Hornsey Road in Islington and less than a mile from our office. The owner of the house had died in the local hospital the previous day. We had been asked to attend, as there were 'a lot of birds in the house' requiring attention and removal. As I pulled up, a man who had been sitting on the low wall in front of the house, got up to greet me.

'Come inside mate. You're not going to believe this. It's like something from a horror film,' he said.

He languidly approached the front door and then stepped aside. I could make out a wry smile on his face, and he was obviously hiding something from me and didn't want to ruin the surprise. In many respects, I was pleased that he hadn't told me what lay beyond the front door, as I would not have believed him.

'There you go mate, take a gander at that. I'll wait here if you don't mind.'

Intrigued I walked past him and through the door. A strong smell of ammonia hit me with such a force that I nearly gagged and fell backwards. My eyes were stinging with the fumes. I opened the first door off the hallway and immediately heard a crescendo of flapping wings and screeching, as though some giant mythical bird was inside; it was quite unnerving. I poked my head round the door and was forced to duck as several pigeons flew at my face. The smell was even more overpowering and I began choking from all the dust blown up by their flapping wings. I quickly shut the door and, when my choking and coughing was under control, I tentatively had another look. I could not believe my eyes and thought the ammonia was giving me hallucinations. I had been expecting to collect a few budgerigars and I was totally unprepared for what I was seeing. The room was a mass of pigeons and, worse than that, the whole room was covered in bird mess. Not the odd bit of soiling, but masses of it, up to six inches deep in places. It covered the few pieces of furniture and the whole floor like a blanket of discoloured snow. There were stacks of cardboard boxes in the room, containing who knows what, which were all covered in inches of greenish white excreta, forming snow drift like formations, on which dozens of pigeons were sitting and standing. There were a scattering of bowls of food and water, out of which some birds were eating. It must have taken years for all the muck to have built up.

I closed the door and moved to the next room. It was just the same as were all the rooms upstairs. No wonder the man who had let me in hadn't tried to explain what to expect. He was right; I would not have believed him. It was like something from a horror film. There must have been hundreds of pigeons in the house, collected over a period of years and allowed to breed indiscriminately. How anyone could have lived in such a state I do not know. I thankfully fled the house and went outside to where the man was sitting on the wall smoking. He could obviously tell from my face how shocked I was.

'Told you, didn't I? Bet you haven't seen anything like it, have you?' he grinned.

'No, you're certainly right, I haven't,' I replied.

'What are you going to do then?' he asked.

'I'll have to feed and water them over the weekend and then see what can be done on Monday. Have you a spare key?'

'Certainly have, and you can help yourself. Let me know what the plan is on Monday.' I returned to the hospital and described the scene to my disbelieving colleague. He then went to take a look for himself, and to feed and water the birds.

There were hundreds of pigeons in the house

On the Monday a group of us returned to the house armed with nets, baskets, masks and Wellington boots. Every room was full of black, brown, white, grey and multi-coloured pigeons. Each room had walls of bare plaster or peeling wallpaper. All the furniture and assorted rubbish was encrusted with layers of white and grey excreta. We spent several hours wading through the drifts of bird muck, fought our way round piles of unrecognisable encrusted furniture, wrestled with hundreds of panicky birds and peered through showers of feathers and dust floating up from the floor. Occasionally, we had to retreat to the fresh air to cool down, as it was unbelievably hot work trying to catch them. Gradually, we began to make headway and cleared each room in turn. We kept a tally of the number we caught. We ran out of baskets and boxes at one point and had to off load some of the birds at the hospital, returning to start all over again. Eventually they were all secured and the final count was 402! We returned to the hospital where we began the long job of checking their health. They were removed individually from the boxes and baskets and examined, before being placed into different cages depending on their state of health. Due to inbreeding, many had bad deformities, and large numbers were suffering from a variety of injuries and ailments. Many had to be humanely put to sleep and the remainder were transported to one of the RSPCA Animal Homes, to be kept until their fate was decided by the deceased owner's family or Solicitor. In the weeks that followed, several more pigeons were put to sleep or died, but eventually some survived and were found new homes.

*   *   *

Meanwhile, back at the hospital, owners poured in with their pets requiring first aid. The summer months were the busiest time for dogs and cats suffering minor injuries, and these were mainly caused through play and walks in the park. Amongst those arriving, were limping dogs suffering very sore and swollen paws caused by a grass seed, picked up during a run in long grass. Small pointed grass seeds are like tiny arrows and have a habit of working their way under the tender skin between the toes. The dog finds this very irritating and licks and chews the paw turning it into a pus filled sore. I always felt so sorry for them in this state, as it must have driven them mad. It is always a good idea to clean their paws after a run or walk in summer grass to avoid this condition.

Often owners turned up with their pets that had been energetically chasing a wasp or bee, only to catch it in their mouth and suffer a sting. If an owner had not actually seen the chase, the first they were aware that anything was wrong, was when the animal suddenly started pawing at its mouth, salivating and rubbing its face along the floor. Bees more often than not left their sting behind, but wasps tended not to. It was imperative to establish when possible which insect had caused the problem. Leaving a sting sac in situ can be dangerous for the animal. If it turned out to be a bee sting, the right procedure was to try to find the sac. This was easier said than done, as opening a dog's sore mouth, and then trying to spot it was difficult. Even when I found the sac it was not easy to remove it with tweezers, as I had to be careful to grasp it at the neck otherwise more venom was squeezed in which made matters worse.

As with humans, stings can be dangerous. Many animals reacted badly and even collapsed and went into shock. Some can get spectacular swelling of the face, which is very alarming for an owner, although not necessarily dangerous. If stung in the throat though, the swelling can cause difficulty in breathing, which can be serious. On the telephone we offered first aid advising owners not to panic, but to wash the mouth of the animal out with a mixture of bicarbonate of soda and water. If the sting was on the body then it had to be washed with surgical spirit. Ice packs can be used to help reduce the swelling. The pain and swelling will often subside given time so we always advised waiting for a while before rushing to a vet for an antihistamine injection and treatment for shock.

Young cats and kittens often managed to get sewing thread or a needle stuck in their throat or mouth. They would find a discarded needle and thread on the carpet and then play with it only to end up swallowing it. Again, it was an awkward procedure to open the mouth and ascertain where it was lodged. Sometimes it was a simple procedure to pull it out with a pair of forceps, but if it was right down the throat, then the animal required admitting to the hospital for the vet to administer an anaesthetic. Cats also arrived with elastic bands caught round their tongues or teeth in a similar way. On occasions animals can get electrocuted. This happens when puppies and kittens chew on electrical wire whilst playing. The result is burns to the mouth, gums and paws, which is really painful and uncomfortable.

Both dogs and cats can pick up bones, usually chicken or chop bones, which can get wedged in the mouth. It is common for some owners to give their dogs a bone to chew on, which is always a mistake, as a splinter can get lodged between the back teeth and the roof of the mouth. The dog immediately starts to retch, gag and cough due to the discomfort and paws at its open mouth trying to remove the bone. It is then a question of holding the jaws apart, whilst, with a pair of forceps or tweezers, attempting to dislodge the bone fragment without dropping it down the dog's throat.

This was never an easy job and at least an extra pair of hands was required. All these ailments arrived at the door at some stage and required our attention.

*   *   *

In the summer there was nothing like being called to a London park on a hot sunny afternoon, particularly if it involved mucking about on a lake or pond to rescue a duck or swan. I was called out to Finsbury Park to do just that, but it didn't involve either ducks or swans.

The park was just up the road from the hospital and, as I turned in, I could see that it was packed with people. There were families playing ball and picnicking, couples sunbathing, lads playing football and the less energetic just sitting and reading. An RSPCA van always turned a few heads and I was watched as I headed towards the lake, which was packed with boats. A park employee met me.

'Sorry to call you out on a weekend,' he apologised.

'No problem. I'm working anyway and it's great to be out on a day like this,' I replied.

'Several people have spotted a cat on the island. I haven't seen it myself and cannot really fathom out how one could have got over there,' he reported.

'Well I must admit that it is unusual for cats to swim and there is no reason for one to want to go over there. Are you sure it isn't someone having a joke?' I asked.

'I don't think so, as several different people have reported it.'

'Have you any idea what colour the cat is?'

'Apparently it is tabby coloured,' said the park ranger.

'It will be well camouflaged then. I suppose I had better take a look. Have you got a boat I can get over there on?'

'I'll take you over if you like,' volunteered the attendant.

'Even better, as my rowing isn't that great.'

We clambered into a small wooden dinghy and headed for the island. I sat in the bow as he did all the hard work, thinking this is the life. I could not think of any better job to be doing on a hot Saturday afternoon. We reached the island and I clambered off. It was not a big island, but it was very overgrown and there were plenty of ducks around, which fled at my arrival. I crawled around almost on my hands and knees, but could not spot a cat. There was no way I could cover the whole island so I retreated to the dinghy.

'No sign I'm afraid, but how about a row round the island while I see if I can spot it,' I suggested.

The park attendant was quite willing, so I settled back in the bow and enjoyed the sunshine whilst peering at the overgrown bank. After a circuit we had not spotted the elusive cat.

'Still no sign, but if he is there it will need rescuing as I can't see it making its way back without help. I'll go back to base and come back later today with a trap and set it overnight.'

Later that afternoon I returned with the trap. This is a really handy piece of equipment, which is simple, humane and effective at catching cats without causing too much distress to the animal. It is a metal cage with a metal plate at one end on which you place food. There is a mechanism, which lifts the plate at an angle and is connected to a rod, which holds up the entry door. When the cat enters the cage, any weight or movement on the plate pulls the metal rod, releasing the spring-loaded door behind the animal and shutting it in. Another metal bar drops down across the door stopping it from pushing its way out. We used these traps in all kinds of situations to rescue wild or timid cats that refuse to be rescued from a tight spot. We returned to the island and I set the trap under a bush with some nice smelly sardines, the odour of which I hoped would permeate round the island and entice it in.

Next morning I returned and long before I reached the trap, I could hear the door rattling which was a sure sign I had been successful. I crawled under the bush to be confronted by a wild-eyed tabby feverishly trying to push the door open. On seeing me, it panicked and spun round several times, as I dragged the trap towards me, making it difficult to carry the cage back to the dinghy.

'Success,' I shouted to the ranger.

'So there was a cat there after all,' he smiled.

'Yes, our efforts were not in vain.'

I got back onto the boat with difficulty, as the cat was still intent on evacuating the cage and was causing the trap and the boat to rock violently. Finally, I managed to sit down with the trap on my knees and I took a close look at him. He was quite a large tabby tom with a white chin and it was difficult to assess whether he was just frightened or whether he was a wild stray. I took him back to the hospital where after a day or so he calmed down and became quite affectionate. How he got onto the island remains a mystery. After a week at the hospital, he had not been claimed, so he was transported to one of our re-homing centres, where two weeks later he was found a home.

* * *

While the nurse attended to the first aid incidents, we were answering the telephone. We would be fighting off owners who wanted to rush up to the hospital with their sick pets. We listened to their description of the symptoms and tried to offer advice. More often than not, this was a delaying tactic, as at some stage during the weekend, we ended up asking them to bring their pet in to one of the emergency surgeries. Some of the ailments were not urgent and we could advise first aid until Monday morning.

People would also be arriving unannounced at the reception desk, often with strange requests: you had to be prepared for anything.

*   *   *

My colleague Nick had just gone upstairs to make a cup of tea and I was busily giving advice to an owner on the telephone. An obviously agitated man appeared in the doorway of the office, hopping from one foot to the other and trying to gain my attention. I signalled to him to hold on and I continued my conversation. I could see out of the corner of my eye that he was getting more anxious by the minute and presumed he must have a seriously injured animal in his car so I ended the telephone conversation.

'Can I help you?' I asked.

'I have got a stray Gerbil in my car and hoped you would take it in', he answered.

'Sure, bring it in'.

'Well there's a problem I'm afraid. On the journey here, the Gerbil has managed to escape out of the box I put in the boot.'

'Oh I see, that could be a big problem. I'll come out with you and take a look.'

I followed the man to his car boot, squatted down, gingerly lifted the door slightly and peered into the gloom. As nothing rushed out, I opened it slightly wider to allow more light to penetrate. I could not see any sign of the small rat like animal, so with the door fully open, I tentatively moved the small cardboard box and some of the contents of the boot. It was at this point that a large furry creature dived underneath some bags, giving me a shock in the process. This was a lot larger than the Gerbil I was expecting, so I hastily withdrew my arm and quickly slammed the door.

'Have you got it?' asked the man.

'Are you sure it was a Gerbil?'

'Well the policeman said it was'.

'Hang on a minute, what policeman?'

'The policeman we called in after we found it in our bedroom this morning.'

'I think you had better start at the beginning and explain what has been going on'.

'Well, my wife and I woke up this morning and found it crawling round the room. She spotted it first and screamed frightening the life out of me. I trapped it under a box and called the police. They came, said it was a Gerbil and suggested bringing it here.'

At this point, Nick, who having made the tea, and was wondering why I was letting it get cold, had wandered out to discover what was happening.

'Got a problem?' he asked.

I quickly explained the situation and once I had convinced him that we had some strange creature in the car, asked him to bring out a pair of gloves and a basket. When he returned, the nurse was accompanying him to join in the fun. While Nick slowly opened the boot, I put the gloves on and then gently started searching. On moving a sack out of the way, I suddenly saw two large black eyes peering at me from a cat like face. Before I had a chance to react, the animal disappeared into a recess by the rear wheel.

'What was it?' Nick asked.

'I have no idea.'

We then slowly and methodically emptied the boot, removed the spare wheel and basically stripped everything out. Having still not located the fugitive we had a little meeting.

'Where on earth is it? I'm sure it did not get passed us and must still be in the car,' I stated.

'Time for drastic action I think,' said Nick, 'we'll have to start looking in the car under the seats.'

We opened three of the doors and with the help of the nurse, thoroughly searched inside without success. With the owner's reluctant permission, we proceeded to remove the back seat. After a lot of tugging, pushing and ominous sounds of ripping it came out, but there was still no sign of the escapee. Scratching our heads somewhat we went back to looking in the boot. I suddenly spotted a slight movement and in a tiny recess behind the wheel arch, I could see some grey fur. In such a confined space, all I could grab hold of was a pinch of the fur, which did not please the creature. After several attempts, I located a tail and then had to wrench the poor thing out of the space it was wedged in. It appeared into the daylight and clamped its tiny jaws onto my gloved finger. I could feel the small needle like teeth penetrating the glove so I quickly plonked him into the basket. We then all stood round and got our first good look at the giant 'Gerbil'. We soon identified him as a Bushbaby, which must have been an escaped pet and somehow found its way into the man's bedroom looking for warmth and security. We kept him in a basket in the office and he soon recovered from the trauma of his escapade. He turned out to be very tame and quickly made himself at home, choosing to lounge on the telephone making it awkward for us. Following a newspaper appeal, he was eventually repatriated with his owner.

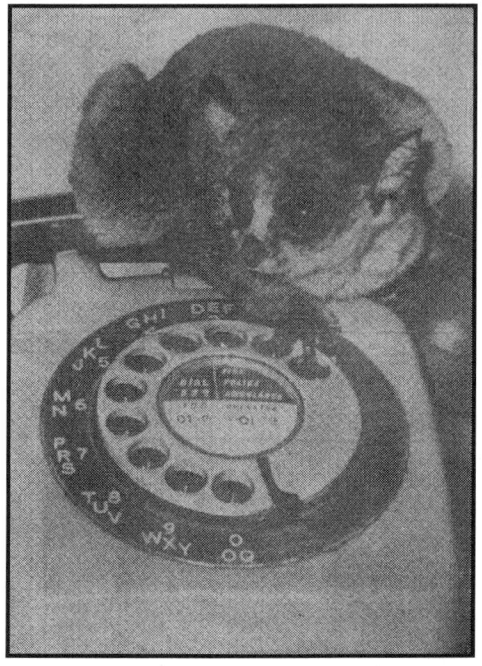

He soon made himself at home in the office.

Saturday was always the difficult day in regard to answering the telephone from owners with sick animals. During the week, we knew that we only had to stall them overnight and then all the private vets and our hospital had a normal outpatient service to see them. On a Saturday, it could be over 36 hours until a vet opened for normal service. The vet arrived at seven o'clock and examined any animals we had admitted before examining the patients we had asked in. If they were all genuine emergencies then we could breathe a sigh of relief and congratulate ourselves. If several were not emergencies, then he might have a little moan at us, but it was impossible to be able to be right all the time and I believe they realised this.

At midnight, we would try to get our heads down as early as possible, because we still had another thirty hours or so to go. Mostly we managed to get some sleep, but there were always those nights when our assistance was required.

*   *   *

It was three o'clock on a decidedly cold November morning and as I stepped out of the van my breath joined forces with the encroaching mist. I had just driven from our base right out to a suburban area of north London called Arnos Grove, in very quick time. I got out and closed the door and, without warning, an eerie shrill scream echoed from the house I had parked outside. It sent a shiver down my whole body and conjured up Jack the Ripper and Hounds of the Baskerville stories. The distressed whimpering sounds that followed though were definitely that of a puppy. I then knew I was in the right place.

Twenty minutes earlier the telephone had rung waking both of us. From my snug position in the top bunk, I had heard my colleague Tom, in the bottom bunk, groan then fumble about in the dark for the table lamp switch. In the dull light, he had found the telephone and I heard him say: 'Good morning, Emergency Service, how can I help?' There was then a long silence as Tom listened to the caller and I prayed that I wouldn't have to relinquish my nice warm sleeping bag. After a couple of minutes, I heard my colleague mutter that heart-sinking phrase 'we'll be there straight away.'

'I have got a call for you,' he smirked.

'Who on earth is up at this time of the morning?' I moaned as I struggled free from my sleeping bag. I peered at my watch in the gloom and waited for the dial to come into focus.

'It's nearly three in the morning,' I complained.

'I know' he said gleefully 'I'm so pleased you are driving tonight and I am answering the phone'.

'Yeah, very funny, what's it all about?'

'A very distressed Mrs Simpson says her puppy has managed to catch its mouth on a tack and is nailed to the floor!'

'You are kidding.'

'Honestly that is what she said. She was too upset to give any other details. Don't wake me up when you get back, will you.'

'I hope the phone never stops ringing while I'm away,' I growled.

I staggered through the hospital slowly waking myself up. Once fully awake and outside in the cold I couldn't wait to get going as this was the part of the job I really enjoyed. I relished these journeys through the streets of London in the early hours. This was the time of night I loved working in London as I had the city virtually to myself. Devoid of pedestrians and traffic, it was as though aliens had arrived and everyone had vacated the city. Back in the 1970's, London was much quieter in the early hours as there were few nightclubs or twenty-four hour takeaways, convenience stores and garages to keep everyone up. It was also mostly empty of police officers and speed cameras and I revelled in speeding through the deserted streets, slowing down at traffic lights and carefully running the red lights. You could drive across London in a quarter of the time it took you during the day. I made great time getting to Arnos Grove.

I found the house and hurried to the front door, intrigued to find out how a puppy could get its mouth nailed to a floor. I rang the doorbell and a young woman who had obviously been crying, opened the door. As she led me through a room empty of furniture or furnishings there was another heartrending scream from nearby.

'The puppy is in the kitchen and my husband is with her. She is only eight weeks old and we have only had her for a few days.'

'I understand the puppy has managed to get its mouth caught on a nail.'

'So my husband says. I haven't seen her, but she keeps screaming in pain. It is very upsetting. We are at our wits end. We didn't know who to call, so we rang the Police. They couldn't help, but suggested calling you. Thank you for coming so quickly.'

At this point, a man appeared at an open window of the room and climbed in giving me a start.

'This is my husband.'

'It is really good of you to come. Sorry about the window, but we can't open the kitchen door because of our pup,' he said.

'No problem, but I am a bit confused as to what is going on,' I said.

'Sorry, let me explain. We only moved into the house a couple of days ago and we have no carpets down and many floorboards up in the house. We were worried the puppy might chew exposed wires or get stuck so we decided it was better to shut her in the kitchen for the night, as there are no holes there. She must have been scrabbling at the bottom of the door to get out and has got her mouth caught on an exposed tack in the floorboard just the other side of the door. Her screams obviously woke us up.'

'Can I see?' I asked.

'Of course.' he answered and climbed back out of the window. 'Follow me.'

I followed him and he led me through the back door into the kitchen. Glass crackled underfoot.

'Sorry about the mess, but I had to break the glass in the back door to get it open.'

On entering the kitchen, the puppy saw us and uttered another shrill scream. I looked down to see a tiny bundle of grey and white fur. It was a very young Old English Sheepdog. I knelt down by the puppy and gently touched her head. She let out yet another ear-piercing scream, which made me jump.

'Interesting,' I said 'this is definitely another first for me. She'll wake the whole street up at this rate and somebody will probably telephone the RSPCA reporting you of cruelty.'

I lay on the floor so that I could get a close look. I gingerly tried to move her head and was ready for the scream this time. I managed to see that she had the very sensitive fleshy part of her lower lip caught round the head of a tack. I felt very sorry for her, as it must have been so painful. I was stuck for an idea with this one, as I couldn't for the life of me formulate a plan of releasing her without causing great pain or injury. I decided to make the decision of calling out our duty vet. This was always a last option and rarely done as they had already worked during the day and when on call, had to be woken up at home. I knew the vet on duty that night had only been with us a couple of weeks, didn't know London very well, and was not familiar with the antics of the night emergency staff. I informed the owners of my plan and took great pleasure waking my colleague. I decided it would be quicker for me to return to the hospital to meet her there and then drive her back to the scene, as she wasn't sure where Arnos Grove was. This was great fun for me as it allowed me two very fast journeys through the empty streets. She seemed to take it all in her stride and didn't appear put out at being roused at three in the morning, driven at breakneck speed across London and then negotiating a window and smashed back door to be confronted by a puppy nailed to a kitchen floor.

She decided to give her a mild anaesthetic, which in fact virtually knocked the puppy unconscious. We were laying full length on the floor either side of the puppy and while I held and slightly lifted the head, the vet made a small incision to cut the lip free. The kitchen door was opened and the distraught wife was united with her pet. The owners were almost in a state of collapse after the traumatic events of the night and they decided to allow us to take the puppy back to the hospital to sleep off the sedation. It was now five-thirty in the morning, and being exhausted, I drove more sedately back to the hospital. It had been a long night for all of us and it wasn't worth trying to get any sleep, as the first staff would be arriving in less than two hours, so we sat in the night room with the puppy reflecting on the night's events over a coffee.

3:

Cats in Trouble

Passers-by were quite curious to discover why a man in uniform was on his hands and knees with his ear to a storm drain, while two Nuns stood over him watching intently. Once again, I had been called out to yet another bizarre situation. Outside a Convent in Colebrooke Row, a quiet street off the Angel Islington, meowing had been heard echoing up from a drain by the side of the pavement. Two of the metal bars that should have been protecting the opening were missing.

I made some silly cat noises, as one does in these situations and I was immediately answered by the pathetic, unmistakably muffled cries of a cat. I put my arm into the drain and found that the pipe went for about a foot or so in a horizontal direction and then disappeared vertically and the cat must have slid down this part. I got up and looked around for inspiration. The two Nuns looked at me expectantly and I gave them a nonchalant smile, as though I was confronted with such a situation every day. I informed them that I was popping round to Islington Town Hall to see who was responsible for the drain. It was only round the corner and I was there in a few minutes. A good-looking, smiling receptionist who was both surprised and concerned to hear of the plight of the cat greeted me. She got on the telephone immediately and within minutes, she had arranged for someone from the sewerage and drainage department to come along as soon as possible. I thanked her profusely and went back to the two Nuns giving them the good news. The receptionist was as good as her word and only twenty minutes later, a huge Drainage Department van pulled up. Four men jumped out, led by a portly man who introduced himself as Bert the foreman. Now Bert was a quintessentially salt of the earth, rough and ready, no nonsense East End worker and union man to boot. He was probably not the type of man to get on the wrong side of, but he was jolly, crude and sincere and took over the situation straight away, once he was convinced that there was a "situation".

'Right lads, let's have a bit o' hush so I can see if this 'ere cat is really 'ere.' Bert had some difficulty getting on his hands and knees, and after a few bizarre cat noises, he too was answered.

'He's in there lads,' he beamed, proud that his cat imitation had elicited a response, but then realising the seriousness of the cat's plight, his face turned to concern. Bert stood contemplating for a while obviously considering a plan of action. He was soon to move heaven and half of Colebrooke Row in his quest to rescue the poor "bleedin" cat. He was quick to point out that he didn't really like cats, but he couldn't leave the "poor beggar" to die. In fact, it soon became an obsession with him.

I stood there while his three mates all took turns to make equally peculiar noises to prove to themselves that there was a cat down there. In an effort to hurry things up, I asked what we should do next.

'It won't take long mate. See the pipe runs horizontal like for a few feet before dropping like and he's probably in the horizontal bit. Easy it is. We'll just lift the top plate off and there we are.'

'Get us the key, Jack mate,' said Bert full of confidence. I didn't have the heart to tell him that I had already checked that part with my arm and the cat was further down. The iron cover was duly removed and everyone cracked their heads as they leaned forward at the same time to gaze in. I was imagining it to be wide, but it was only some eight inches in diameter. Bert borrowed my torch and soon discovered that it was empty.

'Poor beggar must have slipped right into the blinking sewer,' exclaimed the ever-eloquent Bert.

There followed what was to become the ritual of the whole rescue: each of the workmen taking turns to look down the hole, exclaim and swear and then enter into a convoluted discussion.

'What does that mean?' I asked.

'It means it's time for a cuppa and a little conflab', answered Bert, 'Put the kettle on Harry.'

I stood incredulous as they all trooped into the back of their van, which was the size of a removal lorry. I was soon to realise that you could not hurry this lot and to keep on the right side of them it was wise not to try. At their insistence, I joined them in the back and I was amazed to see that it was kitted out like a caravan, with bunks, table and chairs and a fully equipped kitchen. A home from home as Bert put it. I soon had a mug of tea in my hand. The Nuns came out to enquire about the progress of the rescue and Bert became very reverent and toned his language down while he explained what was happening. He then turned to me.

'Sorry about the delay mate, but this 'ere needs some discussion like, as it's going to be difficult.'

'Cat could be anywhere if it's reached the sewer,' commented Harry.

'Nah, it can't be too far or we couldn't hear it,' said Jack.

'Good point, but how are we going to get to it without digging up 'alf the road,' pondered Bert.

'How about approaching from the sewer?' I asked hopefully, with visions of wading through huge dank tunnels filled with rats and God knows what.

'Pipe's only a couple of feet wide down there.'

There were a few minutes of silence while everyone gave the problem serious consideration. Bert broke the silence.

'Nah, it's no good. We'll have to dig up the road where the pipe goes down,' he said.

'You are willing to do that?' I asked.

'No problem,' laughed Bert. 'We don't have the equipment to dig that far down so I'll have to call in contractors for that - it's no skin off our noses.'

He said it would take time to arrange things with his boss, so I left them to another cup of tea and went off to do some other jobs, which were piling up. When I returned, I found two men setting up a pneumatic drill and Bert pacing up and down trying to estimate the precise spot to drill down. One of the contractors was none too happy and almost hostile about having to drill a hole to rescue a cat. This was not going down too well with Bert and when, at one point, the contractor commented about leaving it there to die, he rankled. He had to be restrained from almost thumping the man and had to be placated with another cuppa. From then on, the atmosphere between the two sets of workers was rather frosty to say the least.

Bert had judged the position perfectly and the contractors soon broke through. Bert put down his umpteenth cup of tea, having earlier taken great pleasure in not offering the contractors one. Pieces of rubble and debris had fallen down the hole as the drill broke through. The contractors climbed out for a smoke, while Bert and I peered down the pipe. He gave the contractors a murderous look and swore at them for not being more careful as the bottom was full of rubble. He called for silence and repeated his cat imitation. There was no reply. In fact, none of us had heard it since that first encounter. Bert was obviously seriously concerned about the health of the animal and looked at me gravely.

'What next?' I asked.

He explained that the vertical piece dropped six or seven feet before making a right-angled turn and running horizontally again to the sewer. He presumed the cat was at the bottom covered in rubble or had taken fright and entered the sewer. We were all very despondent, but we did our best to gently remove what rubble we could reach. At this point, the boss of the contractors arrived and announced they were off to lunch. Bert was livid at them "running out on us" and after some heated words, he managed to talk one of them into staying to help. Soon after, the Borough Surveyor turned up to see what had been tying up one of his teams all morning. Although he was very sorry to hear of the plight of the cat, he could not allow our efforts to continue much longer. He told Bert that the drain had to be cleared and repaired regardless of whether it was alive or dead and ordered him to pour a bucket of water down to try and clear it. A very solemn Bert climbed into the hole, and with a heavy heart, he poured the water in. Harry appeared with an industrial size plunger and proceeded to ram it up and down a few times before removing it with a loud squelch.

Then everything seemed to happen at once. Harry literally vaulted backwards with a loud cry and landed at our feet almost giving Bert a seizure. It was several seconds before Harry could tell us the reason for his athletic feat. Apparently, as he removed the plunger, the suction had drawn the cat half way up the pipe. The unexpected shock of seeing the animal had frightened him into his backward flip. We all made a mad scramble to look down the hole before Bert shouted at us to get out as we were kicking more debris in. We could definitely hear the pitiful cries again and we carefully peered down. Every few seconds we could see the head of a small kitten appear at the bend as it tried to scramble up to the light and fresh air.

'Well I'll be blowed,' exclaimed Bert 'It's bleedin' amazing. It's still alive.'

He was almost overcome with joy and I half expected him to do a jig in celebration. There were smiles all round. Unfortunately though, the kitten was still six feet underground at the bottom of a narrow pipe. For the first time Bert was getting anxious.

'It will take hours to dig down that far even if we were allowed to,' he moaned.

'I have an idea,' I said and everyone looked round expectantly.

I went to my van and returned with the ever useful grasper. 'It's not long enough, but if we could attach an extra bit of handle and rope we might be able to reach down,' I suggested.

'Good idea!' exclaimed Bert 'Harry, get some tape and a broom handle from the van.'

Harry disappeared into the van and appeared a few seconds later carrying a broom and a roll of thick tape.

'Like the boy scouts we are,' smiled Bert.

Harry broke the broom-head off the handle and with the help of Bert managed to strap the handle to the pole. One of the other men appeared with a length of thin cord and attached it. We now had a pole long enough to poke down and everyone was getting very excited, but we still had some problems. When I laid headfirst in the hole and gently threaded the pole down I could not get the leverage to pull the rope at the same time, so Harry volunteered to pull it from above me, but he couldn't see when the kitten had it's head through the loop.

'I'll tell you what, I will shout when the kitten has its head in the right position and you can give the rope a tug,' I told Harry.

Harry was worried that if he pulled it too strongly he would strangle the kitten. It was by now though, a do or die situation, and we were all getting affected by the plaintive cries of the poor creature far below. The first few attempts were a failure, as the tentative reactions of Harry, who was now paranoid about strangling the "little mite" as he called it, were not quick enough. A very nervous Bert hovered above us giving encouragement, but it was very tense. The head kept appearing and disappearing, but finally the kitten grabbed the rope with a paw and scrambled up slightly further. I shouted, Harry gave a tug and the noose closed round the kitten's leg and neck. I screamed to Harry to pull up the pole as quickly as he could, which he did. A hissing sodden matt of fur flew past my head and I scrambled out of the hole and pounced on it. I held the poor little thing to my chest. It was terrified and tried to scratch me to escape. I quickly put it in a basket that I had optimistically placed next to the hole in readiness. The poor creature was almost unrecognisable as a kitten. Its fur was plastered to its skinny body and large eyes, which appeared out of proportion to its body, peered round at us. Bert was in raptures and stood shaking his head and saying 'It's a bleedin' miracle, that's wot it is'.

Everyone flopped to the ground round the basket overcome by the emotional exhaustion of the last few minutes. I sat there for a while so that everyone could watch and make comforting noises at the kitten they had just expended so much time and energy to rescue. I thought it was only right they should be able to revel in the moment. As I returned to my van, I looked over my shoulder to see Bert excitedly and profanely holding forth about the last few moments of the incredible rescue. It was these little scenarios, which made doing the job so wonderful and enjoyable.

*   *   *

Cats are extremely intelligent animals and are expert climbers, but even with these attributes, they are always getting into trouble. Their downfall is the fact that they love to roam and have a very inquisitive nature. Any chance to climb onto a roof or investigate an opening or dark space is too much to ignore. Stalking mice and birds is a natural passion and can lead them into all sorts of difficulties, as is the chance to sneak in somewhere in search of food.

It is probably not a surprise then that we received regular calls to them stuck on roofs, ledges, and trees and trapped in buildings or confined spaces. My first ever rescue was to a cat sitting on a third floor window ledge of a derelict house. I am not quite sure whether she had jumped down from the roof or had squeezed through a broken corner of the window glass, but she had been pathetically calling down to the market stall holders and passers-by in the street all morning. I had arrived with my ladder full of expectation and excitement. I was greeted in the Bethnal Green street by good-humoured locals who helped me put the ladder up. With a crowd of onlookers encouraging me, I had climbed up, grasped the cat, which then clung round my neck and descended to tongue in cheek applause and congratulation. I had begun my animal rescue career successfully and loved every minute of it.

Trees were the most common place to become "stuck". Once a cat has reached a dizzy height, some appear to lose the will or expertise to find a way down. This was often the case with a kitten or young cat with no experience. One thing is certain: they much prefer to jump down from a height and cannot seem to get their head round the procedure of coming down backwards.

Rescuing them from trees or other high places was a relatively simple operation back then. I strapped a ladder to the roof of the van, drove to the incident and whacked the ladder against the tree or building making as much noise as possible in the hope that the cat would run down. If that failed, I climbed up with one hand, often wearing a thick glove and carrying a basket in the other. No hard hat, no harness, no safety ropes, no assistance and no sign of Health and Safety Regulations. I sweated and slipped; I suffered cuts and bruises; and was sometimes scratched and bitten.

Most cats did not appreciate being rescued, as the sight of a rescuer often terrified them. They would retreat further up the tree or further along the branch making it more dangerous for all concerned. When I had reached a cat and tried to remove its grip, the animal often struggled or lashed out, which was no fun when precariously perched thirty feet or more up. Once

I had hold of the animal, it usually clung on to me for all it was worth.

If I was unable to rescue the animal, I just reverted to plan B and called the Fire Brigade. I remember on one occasion being half way up a tree attempting to rescue a cat that had supposedly been up there four days. The large black tom had been watching my antics with great interest and then a little old woman appeared at the foot of the tree.

'I've been watching you from my kitchen window. What are you doing?' she enquired.

I looked down at her with perspiration dripping from my face.

'I'm trying to rescue this cat,' I replied jerking my head in the direction of the cat some ten feet above me.

'Why are you trying to get it down,' she persisted.

I was beginning to get irritated with her.

'Because it is stuck and cannot get down on its own.'

'Oh yes it can,' she insisted.

'What do you mean?'

'He's mine and he goes up there every day unless it's raining and then in the evening he comes down to me to be fed. I think he goes off to see his girlfriends after that. He's a naughty boy', she chuckled. With that, she went back into her house shaking her head at the fool I obviously was. The cat continued to look benignly down at me with just the hint of a smirk.

In a similar scenario, I was half way up a bushy tree trying to force myself between thick branches when a lady strolled nonchalantly over to the bottom of the tree.

'May I ask what you are trying to do?' she said in a prim voice.

I looked down at her rather peeved, "I am trying to rescue a cat that is stuck up here".

'Oh I see. Well I thought I should perhaps point out to you that I saw it scramble down the other side a few minutes ago and disappear into that garden.'

With that, she quietly and slowly walked away. I had spied the cat a few minutes before still at the top, but I had been so intent on my difficult climb without causing myself injury, that I hadn't seen it disappear.

*   *   *

'Well before you say anything young man, there is no way I am sending any of my men up there.' said the officer rather sternly.

'I know what you mean,' I glumly answered.

'Hell, I have never seen a cat up that high before. It must be well over sixty foot or more,' he went on. 'We would never get a ladder high enough.'

This was the second day that I had returned to Woodberry Down Estate off the Seven Sisters Road at Finsbury Park. A young tabby cat named Jeremy had decided to climb up what was probably the tallest tree in North London, situated between a pair of six storey blocks of flats. We had been barraged with telephone calls from the owner of the cat and residents, so the previous afternoon I had gone along to take a look, and on arrival, I had spotted Jeremy half way up this very tall, thin tree sitting on a branch and emitting the odd plaintive meow. As the cat did not appear in imminent danger of falling, I had explained that I would be leaving Jeremy up there to give him a chance to get down on his own. This decision was not greeted favourably by the owner and assembled residents, who gradually became quite aggressive.

There was an agreement between the Fire Brigade and the RSPCA at the time to leave a cat up a tree for at least 48 hours, in order to give it a chance to come down of its own accord. Members of the public, who telephoned them direct, would usually be referred to the Society and we would attend and assess the situation and attempt a rescue ourselves. The theory was that hunger, or possibly bad weather, would give the animal an incentive to come down. It was also because they often wasted their valuable time and resources by attending, only for the cat to take fright. The result of all this was that we became the impartial arbitrators of when, and if, an animal required rescuing. This often put us in an invidious situation as piggy in the middle. We had to weigh up the risks to the animal, and explain any consequences to the owners if they were present.

I felt sorry for them of course, but it was surprising how many got into this kind of trouble and it was impossible to attend them all. There could also be cases where attempting a rescue put the rescuer and the animal's life in danger. Some owners not only expected, but also thought it a right, that they could demand that someone else should risk death or injury and also pay for the rescue of their pets, whilst taking no action themselves. All these factors could turn what appeared to be simple incidents into quite traumatic experiences for all concerned.

That night we were inundated with calls pleading with us to do something and so I had returned the next morning and to my horror, discovered that far from coming down, Jeremy had decided to migrate to the very top of the tree and was swaying in the breeze and looking terrified. It was now obvious that he was in a precarious position, and in danger of falling, so even though he had only been up there twenty-four hours, I decided to intervene. I looked around to see groups of residents staring with menacing looks as the owner approached me again. I knew I had to do something, but it appeared that there was no way the tree could be climbed, no ladder would be long enough and there was not enough space to get a turntable ladder close. I had decided to call the Fire Brigade out anyway in the hope that they might have some miraculous idea. They had arrived within ten minutes and six firemen had trooped over to me. They were all pointing up into the tree with amazement and shaking their heads, which did not look promising.

'It has been up there twenty-four hours, but it is obvious he is not going to make his own way down,' I continued to the Officer.

'I'm sorry, but I don't know if we are going to be able to help you on this occasion my friend,' he said circling the tree and obviously thinking hard.

I was beginning to worry as a large crowd had gathered on hearing and seeing them. They were obviously expecting a rescue and if we packed up and tried to leave, I wasn't sure what would happen. I explained this to him.

'In that case we had better have a word with the owner and do something drastic,' he said more positively.

He proceeded to explain to us his idea.

'My plan is a bit risky and could result in injuring him. I want that understood, but I cannot think of any other way. I plan to send some men up to the roof of the flats with a grappling hook on a long length of rope. We will try to throw the hook into the tree and then shake him down. As a safety measure, we'll have a tarpaulin below to catch him if he falls. It is the only suggestion I have and you'll have to take it or leave it,' he explained.

We placed the onus of the decision onto the owner, who reluctantly agreed and then they went into action. I wasn't at all confident with the plan, but we had to try something, otherwise Jeremy would probably fall anyway and injure himself.

Two firemen disappeared into the flats and a few minutes later appeared on the roof while the others spread a large tarpaulin at the base of the tree. The tree was some thirty feet away from the flats and it took five attempts to get the grappling hook firmly lodged in the upper branches. Once this was done, the rest of us, plus a few onlookers, grabbed hold of the sheet and raised it from the ground in readiness.

The Officer gave the order to start shaking the tree and we held our breath. I could hardly bear to look. Nothing really happened to begin with as the tree was quite large and it took a lot of strength to move it. Another fireman went up to the roof to help his colleagues and with the extra manpower they managed to get the tree to shake slightly which resulted in Jeremy slipping several feet down the trunk where he held on for grim life. So far, so good. They then gave a much harder tug with far more enthusiasm, which caught Jeremy off guard with a disastrous result.

He completely lost his grasp and launched himself away from the tree into free fall. It is at times like this when everything always appears to progress in slow motion. With his legs and claws fully extended and tail swirling and acting as a rudder, he plunged earthwards. Unfortunately, this action also caught all of us off guard. We had believed that if Jeremy did fall he would drop straight down, but now we were standing in the wrong place with the tarpaulin. In a panic, we all made a valiant effort to get underneath him, but only succeeded in tripping each other up and we landed in a heap on the grass. There was a sickening thud as Jeremy hit the ground some four feet away.

I scrambled up and pounced on him in case he ran off, but having fallen some sixty feet he was in no condition to run away and was lying there winded and disorientated and his lack of movement was making me feel sick. I quickly examined him and was overjoyed to see he was breathing and moving his head to look at me. He had a nosebleed, but incredibly appeared to have no broken bones. I knew the cat could have internal injuries, so I said I would rush him back to our hospital. I assured the concerned firefighters, owner and onlookers that everything would be fine and they were all relieved.

Back at the hospital Jeremy was examined and found to have no broken bones, but had split the roof of his mouth and had broken several teeth with the impact of his head hitting the ground. He was severely shocked, but following treatment and two day's rest, he was fit to go home. His owner promised to keep him in for a week or so to recover.

It is astonishing how cats can survive such falls and mercifully, I have only seen it happen on a few occasions. When falling, they are similar to humans in free fall with their four legs out-stretched. They use their legs and tail to keep themselves upright, to help slow their descent down and to actually guide themselves in a certain direction. By doing this, they usually hit the ground on all fours, which helps lessen the impact. Even so, their head still suffers the main injuries such as fractured jaws, split palates and broken teeth.

I thought this would be the last time I met Jeremy, but a week or so later we had another report of a cat up a tree at the same location. Surely, this could not be him again and in the same tree. I drove to the estate with a sinking feeling and as I walked round the corner of the flats, there was Jeremy the tabby cat almost in the same position. I could not believe it. He had obviously not learned from his first experience. I advised the owner that it might prove fatal to try to rescue him the same way as before, even if I could get the Fire Brigade to attend again, which I doubted. I advised leaving him for a while again.

Someone got in touch with the media and they lapped up the story and could not help having a dig at the RSPCA for doing nothing. Jeremy then became quite a celebrity and when a window cleaner volunteered to climb up, the newspapers attended in large numbers to watch him scale the tree with the aid of a safety harness to successfully rescue Jeremy for a second time. To my knowledge this was the last time he ventured up there.

* * *

'Sorry to call you out, but I have been trying to get the cat down for the last hour without success. I have tried tempting it down with food and appealing to it,' I explained to the sub officer.

We were standing below a thin tree in the back garden of a terraced house. We had been using delaying tactics with the owner of the house, but had finally agreed to try to get the cat down. Unfortunately, the tree was more like a sapling and was too thin to climb or safely put a ladder against.

'I have been using my grappling hook and rope to try and shake him down, but I cannot get enough leverage,' I continued.

'Well that seems a pretty good plan to me. With extra hands I reckon we can get the tree to sway,' he suggested and turned to one of his men. 'Get the rest of the lads out the back.'

The fireman disappeared through the house and returned a few minutes later with three others.

'The plan is to throw the hook up there and gently shake the cat down. And I emphasise the gently part otherwise I don't think the RSPCA man will be too pleased,' ordered the Officer.

The assembled firemen smiled and grabbed my grappling hook. After several attempts, they managed to get the hook lodged in the top of the tree while the cat peered nervously down at us, emitting the occasional weak meow.

'Right lads, give it a tug.'

They did this with gusto and the tree shook violently. I could see the cat taken by surprise and slip a couple of feet before grabbing hold with a vengeance. They made several more attempts at shaking him down, but he hung on with grim determination some twenty feet up. One of them tried to climb the tree, but the thin branches gave way under his weight.

'I have an idea if it is OK with you,' said the Officer turning to me. He explained that he thought the tree was thin enough for us to try and actually bend the top right over and near the ground so that either the cat could safely jump or we could get to it. I have to admit I was slightly dubious about this, but agreed that it was worth a try. I had visions of the tree snapping in half or the cat falling. This time all of them grabbed hold of the end of the rope. Like a tug of war team, they heaved and the tree began to bow. When the tree was almost at right angles and success was within reach, we heard the terrible sound of straining wood. All of a sudden, the grappling hook came free, as the branch it was attached to, snapped. Without a word of a lie, the effect was devastating and the tree swung back into place like a catapult; the hapless cat was literally sent into orbit right over the roof of the house and out of sight. We all stood stunned for a moment and couldn't believe our eyes. It did not seem possible. Coming to our senses, we all rushed through the house to the other side. We searched for a long time, but never discovered the cat. We just hoped that he had landed safely. This was one of very few failed rescues.

*   *   *

Abscesses in cats were far more common then, due to the large stray population and the number of un-neutered pets. They are predominately caused during fights when a tooth or claw coated with bacteria penetrates the skin. Infection soon sets in, and if left untreated, pus builds up resulting in a large swelling, which may eventually burst. This can give the impression that the cat has suffered a horrific accident. By the time this happens, the cat will be feeling ill, as it will have a raging temperature, sometimes as high as 105 degrees. The normal course of treatment would be to lance the abscess under an anaesthetic, flush out the infection and then administer a course of antibiotics. This was not always easy when dealing with a wild feral one. If a human is bitten or clawed they can develop blood poisoning or cat scratch fever as it was called. This can be dangerous and several staff were hospitalised with incredibly swollen limbs and fever during their career.

The vast swathes of derelict land resulting from the bombing of London during the Second World War became the home and territories of thousands of cats that had run off terrified, or had been left behind by their fleeing owners. These had been fighting, breeding and dying of disease, unmolested and independent of humans since the War, becoming feral in the process. They were literally living as wild animals with a complete social hierarchy. Magnificent huge males with enlarged heads the size of bowling balls and muscular backs and legs, would fight rivals to keep their harems. Their heads were big as their cheeks enlarged at maturity and hardened up to provide them with protective armour during fights. At some stage though, an opponent would get a lucky strike in and a claw would puncture the skin and tissue. The more cowardly would also get abscesses on their legs and tails as they turned to run away from the victor. Eventually many of the gaping wounds would heal over of their own accord leaving these males covered in battle scars.

Although most of the time they could survive quite adequately on their own, feeding on the large rodent population and raiding houses and bins for scraps, the odd epidemic would often occur amongst them. They became sick with cat flu, were sometimes poisoned, were hit by cars or suffered horrible skin rashes from flea infestations. Catching them was a real struggle as it was impossible to handle them, as they did not appreciate you were trying to help. I have had tremendous battles attempting to hang on to large muscular male feral cats.

If I had them on the end of a grasper they would literally fly up into the air, all four feet grasping the pole in an attempt to loosen the noose and urinate all over me at the same time. Trying to put them into a basket while they jumped around was another nightmare. They would flail their legs and hang on and actually lift the basket up or kick it away. Once in I had to sit or put my foot on the lid to try to lock it, as they would push the lid up. They had phenomenal strength and after a gladiatorial encounter with one, I was exhausted. Mostly I had to rely on traps, but even then, they sometimes used their sheer strength to force their way out by buckling the metal cage door. They kept us busy trying to catch them when they did get into trouble. The only word to describe them was awesome and I had great respect for them.

* * *

'Come in mate. He's in the back garden. In a terrible mess he is. Half his face is missing,' said the old man wringing his hands.

He led me down the dark corridor of his terraced house. I followed with basket, gloves and grasper in my hands: standard equipment for catching an injured cat.

'He must have been hit by a car or attacked by something,' continued the old man in an agitated state.

It was a small brick walled garden with the original outside toilet still in situ. The man pointed towards the back gate.

'He's hiding behind the dustbin there. Terrible state he's in,' he repeated 'made me feel quite queasy when I spotted him as I put the rubbish out. You'll have to put him to sleep I'm sure.'

I was now beginning to wonder what injuries this poor cat was suffering from as, by the description of the old man, he must have been in a real mess. I quietly and tentatively approached the dustbin and then tried to peer behind it. I didn't want to spook the cat and have it running off, although from the man's description I was expecting to find it dead. As I peered over the top of the bin I heard a low growl followed by a hiss and then I spotted a huge tabby and white cat. At first glance it did indeed look as though half his face was missing, but it was soon obvious that he had a massive abscess on the right side of his face which had recently burst open. Flaps of reddened skin were hanging from a gaping livid hole in his cheek and evil smelling pus was dripping out. The old man was right, the poor animal did look in a wretched way, but abscess wounds always look far worse than they are.

I wasn't sure how the cat was going to react to me trying to get hold of him, but when he only weakly attacked my outstretched gloved hand, I felt confident that I could grab him by the scruff. I hated using graspers on those with wounds on their neck or head. With the basket open at my feet, I quickly leaned over and grabbed him before he had a chance to respond. He went into a hissing fit and lashed out with his claws, but before he knew it, he was in the basket with the lid slammed down.

'I told you he was in a bad way,' stated the old man.

I thought twice about trying to explain that the wound was worse than it looked, but I didn't want to disappoint him. After all, he had been good enough to take the trouble to report the cat to us.

'Yes, he is in a bad way, but thanks to you calling us out I'm sure our vet will be able to put him right, so thank you,' I said.

The old man was happy about that and led me back to the van.

*   *   *

Early one evening I was called to Alexandra Palace where a cat was reported trapped on the huge glass dome roof. I couldn't understand how it had managed to get up there. I had been there before and I could picture how high the roof was. The Palace at the time was in full use as an exhibition centre, but only a few years later, in 1980, it was gutted by fire and took a decade to rebuild. It is a huge building, sited on a hill, and was famous for where BBC Television was first broadcast in the 1930's. Somehow and for some reason, this cat had found its way up on to the glass roof and was lying on a girder some seventy odd feet above the ground.

I slowly drove up the steep approach road craning my neck to see if I could spot the daredevil animal. I got out and then had to walk away from the building in an endeavour to see the top of the roof. A nearby family approached me.

Have you seen the cat?' the husband inquired.

I'm afraid I still haven't spotted it.'

'It's half way up the roof there,' he informed me pointing up with his arm.

'Oh yes, I can see him now.'

'I can't believe he is that high up. How are you going to get him down?'

'At this present moment in time I have no idea'.

More people gathered round us and stared up pointing at the dark blob. I had attended many rescues involving cats on roofs and ledges, but for sheer height and spectacle, this surpassed all the others. I had no idea whether it was possible or advisable to try to rescue it. The cat took tentative steps at intervals and then would just peer down at us. It did not appear to know where it was or what to do. I stood and watched for a while and was stared at by people expecting me to do something.

'Are you going up there to rescue it mister', asked one of the man's children.

'We'll see. I am going to get the Fire Brigade to help me.'

'Cor, can we wait and see them?' the young lad asked his father.

I radioed my colleague at base to call them. Ten minutes later a fire tender crawled up the hill with its blue lights flashing much to the enjoyment of the boy beside me. The crew jumped out and looked up towards where all the bystanders were pointing and I could see disbelief on their faces. I half expected them to turn round and depart.

'Before you say anything I can see the predicament,' the sub-officer said to me smiling.

The smile gave me hope that they were willing to help.

'I have to admit that I have no idea how it managed to get up there.' I said.

'It's got to be some kind of record as I have never dealt with a cat on a roof that high up before.'

'Would you be willing to assist? I know it is asking a lot, but I think it is genuinely distressed and could fall if it tries to get down.' I pleaded.

'I'll have to get permission from my control and get my guv'nor and another crew here as it is going to be a bit involved. I'm sure we can do something though.'

They were the magic words I wanted to hear. He went off to make all the arrangements and to sanction it with his boss and the Palace management and staff. The light started to deteriorate and the crowd began to swell with all the activity. I could hear a siren in the distance and very soon, the guv'nor with two rings on his white helmet, arrived in a second tender. He didn't appear to be as sympathetic, which worried me for a while, but after chatting to his subordinate, he gave the go ahead. They decided that it would be too dangerous to attempt to get to the cat from the outside, as it was too high up and dangerous to scale the roof, so the rescue attempt was redeployed indoors. This caused chaos in the building as spectators had to be cordoned clear of all the activity. Everyone was now watching the rescue attempt anxiously.

With the aid of ladders and ropes, the two fire crews managed to get three firemen up onto one of the supporting roof girders and they then bravely crawled along it to the inside of the glass dome, near to where the cat was positioned, watching all the activity with interest. They removed a pane of glass near to where the daredevil feline was crouching. At first, he backed away at the sight of them and they tried to encourage him to come to them. I was standing below screaming under my breath to the cat not to be stupid. Having caused all this mayhem, I did not want him moving further up the roof and making it impossible to save him. After several minutes, he made cautious steps towards the outstretched arm of the fireman, who was lying on the girder with his head outside the opening. His colleagues were hanging onto him and finally he managed to grab hold of the cat, which clung to his tunic, terrified. When they reached ground level I approached with a basket, but the wild-eyed black cat became frightened, and struggled violently, managing to bite the poor rescuer and escape from his grasp. The cat then ran amok amongst the legs of the bystanders, in total panic, and was gone in an instant. We were all stunned for a moment, as we had not anticipated such a disappointing end to all the hard work. The ungrateful cat was never seen again, but it had been an extremely brave and involved rescue and epitomised the lengths they would go to help.

*   *   *

'Are you sure the power is switched off?' I asked with trepidation.

'I'm one hundred per cent sure mate. We always switch it off after the last train.'

I wasn't convinced, but gingerly jumped down from the platform onto the track. I had been called to the Underground Station after the driver of the last train of the night had reported seeing an animal lying between the rails. I had been met at the entrance and escorted down to the platform. It was always rather weird and eerie to wander through an Underground Station after the system had closed down; everywhere was so quiet. No rattling escalators or the whoosh and bang of trains as they entered and exited the tunnels. No sounds of running feet, tannoy announcements and the voices of hundreds of passengers. What sounds you made were amplified and echoed through the still tunnels. It reminded me of a Dr Who episode I had seen when Daleks were roaming the Underground exterminating everybody. I half expected to see one appearing round each corner.

I got hold of my basket and grasper and started to follow the maintenance crew along the tunnel. There was lighting on, but it was too dim to be useful, and so powerful torches lit the way. Whenever I went down these tunnels, I never seemed to be able to walk in a straight line. Even though I had been told that the power in the live rail was off, I still wanted to stay well clear, but I always seemed to veer towards it. It was very unnerving.

'The driver reported seeing it somewhere about here,' stated one of the men.

We all shone our torches in different directions and walked a yard at a time.

'Over here,' shouted one of them.

We went over to where he was shining his torch down to the ground. I could see what looked like a cat trying to squash its body against the sleeper and make itself invisible.

'It's a cat,' he stated.

I crouched down while the workmen lit up the scene. There was a small dark coloured cat curled up and visibly shaking with fear and shock. She lifted her head weakly and looked up at me with dull eyes. She was obviously badly injured, but I could not see what her injuries were. She did not offer any resistance when I gently lifted her up by the scruff of her neck so as not to aggravate any possible internal injuries.

'Ur, it's missing a leg,' shouted the man behind me.

I had a quick look in the light of the torch.

'It's much worse than that,' I said," I'm afraid she has lost most of both hind legs'.

The workmen all literally recoiled at this news.

'Poor little beggar,' said one.

'It must be in agony,' said another.

'It's a shame, poor blighter,' said his colleague.

All the men were extremely sad, and almost in tears, as they took a close look at the lovely dark tabby cat. She had obviously lost a lot of blood and was in deep shock. I gently lowered her into the basket, she didn't struggle or utter a murmur. She seemed resigned to whatever fate faced her.

'Going to put her down mate?' asked one man
'Best thing, eh mate?' said another.

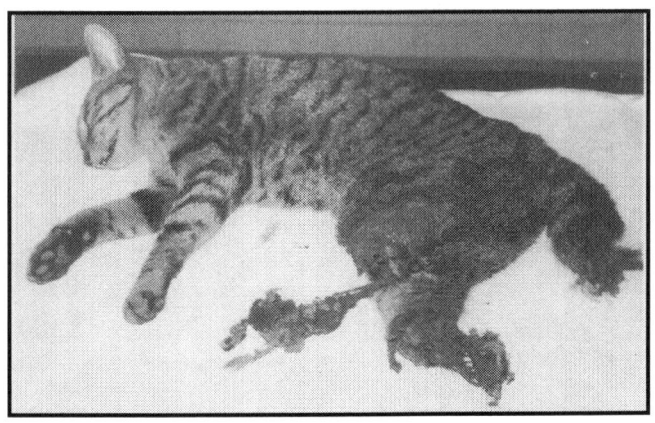

She lifted her head and looked at me with dull eyes

The cat lay there making weak attempts to move. I have to admit that I was really upset. I had come across animals with one severed limb before, but never two. I lifted the basket and I made my zigzag way back to the platform. One of the men tenderly lifted the basket up and then helped me.

'Do you think it's been there a long time?' he asked.
'I think so', I replied.
'It's amazing it lasted so long. It must have been in incredible pain', he commented.

The men were visibly upset and quite shaken and I did not want to put the cat to sleep in front of them. I said my goodbyes, leaving the men in a distressed state, and went back to the ambulance. There I took a closer look and discovered that both legs were severed just below the knee and the tail was severed near the base. The train must have caught the poor cat just as she ran across the line. Amazingly, she had not bled to death, but had laid there all alone with trains thundering over her. With words of comfort, I put her to sleep. Later the duty vet estimated that she must have been lying there for at least 48 hours. It did not bear thinking about. Once again, this incident only proved to me the incredible capacity animals have of absorbing pain and suffering without fuss or obvious reaction. It was all very saddening and something that thankfully did not occur that often.

4:

The Long Weekend – Sunday

It was about nine o'clock on a sunny Sunday morning and although our lazy early morning routine had been ruined, I was enjoying a leisurely drive through the deserted streets heading for the West End. We had just received a call from a very frustrated restaurant owner in Leicester Square, who had a bird trapped in his Pizzeria restaurant which was causing mayhem.

I drove slowly up Coventry Street to where it reached the pedestrian only Leicester Square and soon spied the Pizzeria. I got out of my van and retrieved a net and a basket from the back. As I was in no hurry I strolled across the Square towards the restaurant with the net under my arm. It looked so shabby in the early morning when it was devoid of all the crowds of revellers. At night it was all bright lights and bustle and you did not really notice the rubbish, the grimy paving stones covered in flattened chewing gum and the homeless sleeping on the benches. I reached the restaurant and tapped on the front window. A small Italian man in an agitated state appeared at the door.

'Come in, come in,' he almost begged.

I entered the door and saw a stout red-faced lady frenziedly running around the vast restaurant with a broom held high.

'This is my wife,' he explained. 'We came in this morning to open up and found this pigeon in here. It has caused such a mess all over the tables and chairs. We must get it out as we need to open soon.'

I surveyed the room and sure enough there were a lot of bird droppings and quite a few feathers floating about the place.

'I take it that you have been chasing the pigeon around for quite a while judging by the mess?' I enquired.

'Yes we have. We have kept the front door open and have been chasing it with brooms, but it just flies from one side of the room to the other,' he explained waving his arms from side to side.

The ceiling must have been ten to twelve feet high and the room some sixty feet long. Unfortunately running all round the room near the ceiling there was a ledge on which the pigeon was now perched. There were also light fittings and wooden trellises adorned with plants that the pigeon could make use of. He was peering down at us with a 'what are these crazy people going to do now' look on his face. I only had my hand net on me so I went back to my van for a couple of extension rods. Once back in the restaurant I screwed the cane rods together so that I had a handle some six feet long. The only problem with cane rods is that they are bendy and the pole becomes a little cumbersome.

'Right, I will have a go, but I cannot be responsible for any damage or mess I might cause,' I told the restaurant owner.

'I don't care what you do as long as you get rid of that bird.'

What then followed would have done justice to a Royal Ballet production. I ran, I jumped, I pirouetted and I threw my arms round in vain attempts to get the pigeon into the net. Chairs tipped over, pots of plants tumbled and there was the odd tinkle of broken glass. The pigeon flew from one side of the room to the other, collided with the glass shop-front in a shower of feathers, liberally sprinkled the tables and chairs with droppings in his panic, and cleverly avoided all my attempts to catch him. After five minutes, we both sat panting, me on a chair and he perched back on the ledge. I sat staring at him wondering what to do next and he stared down at me with a 'you're going to have to do better than that mate' expression.

'It's no good. I am going to need some help from you,' I said to the shocked restaurant owners who were standing there surveying the mess.

'What can we do?' they asked in unison.

'If you can get hold of your brooms again and just chase him around so he cannot perch anywhere, I'm sure at some point, he'll fall to the ground or fly past me close enough so that I can get him; you just keep him occupied and don't worry about me.'

This time I climbed up onto a table so that I had more height and reach to swing the net. I gave my accomplices the nod and they bizarrely hurtled round the room screaming in Italian at the tops of their voices and waving the brooms in the air. I was rather taken aback at first as I wasn't anticipating all the screaming, but they soon had the pigeon flying around. The bird flew past me a couple of times, but I missed him. After a few minutes the pigeon started to tire, as did the restaurant owners, but suddenly my adversary landed on a table next to me and I dropped the net over him. I jumped down careful not to dislodge the net and I had him. I quickly popped him into the basket and once again flopped into a chair. My arms were really aching and I was sweating profusely with all the effort. The restaurant owners too had slumped into chairs also exhausted.

'I've got him!,' I exclaimed proud of myself.

The owners just stared at me and then at their wrecked Pizzeria.

'I will take him away and release him. I couldn't have done it without you,' I said, trying to cheer them up.

'Please don't release it anywhere near here,' he pleaded.

I left them to their clearing up. As I wandered back towards my van, I took a little detour into the garden area of the Square, opened the lid of the basket and the pigeon jumped out. He gave himself a shake, gave me a look and wandered off to join his mates, who were busily pecking away at some takeaway scraps.

*   *   *

Sunday mornings were always greeted with a degree of tiredness and dishevelment, dependent upon how many interruptions we had received during the night. In the early hours we might get away without having any telephone calls or call outs if the gods were really with us. More often than not, though, we would have at least a couple of disturbances and sometimes we could have been up all night dealing with an emergency of some kind. We just never knew what was going to transpire, which was part of the attraction of the job for me. I have always hated things being predictable or routine.

With the night over, one of us would volunteer to make the first cup of tea of the day, while the other relaxed a few minutes more. Then the routine was to make a quick check on any patients we had admitted and start cooking breakfast. It was annoying if we happened to receive a call out at this particular juncture, as once the day had kicked off, we often did not get time for breakfast. We would transfer the telephones downstairs to the reception from our night room. The weekend nurses would arrive, and we were all set for another unpredictable day.

Sunday mornings were usually quiet as people recovered from their Saturday nights out. The first telephone calls would come in after ten o'clock and occasionally we would get an early ambulance call. Usually it was a relaxed affair until the vet arrived for the morning emergency surgery at eleven o'clock. Most of the owners who arrived were those we had spoken to during the night and had told to come in. Others brought pets back that had been seen the previous day and required a further check to see if their condition was improving.

When the vet first arrived, he examined the animals we had admitted during the night followed by those we had asked in for the morning surgery. If no emergency operations were required, he disappeared home leaving us to hold the fort again. The volume of telephone calls then increased as more people awoke and other owners wandered arrived with animals requiring first aid as on Saturday.

Late on a Sunday morning, we often received a call from the duty Inspector to attend Club Row market in the depths of the East End. This was a rather dirty, dingy and depressing market held every Sunday morning in Sclater Street and the surrounding small narrow streets running between Bethnal Green Road and Brick Lane. The street on its southern side was lined with arches under the railway line to Shoreditch Station. These cast a shadow over the market and it didn't seem to have the flair and good-natured bustle of other colourful London street markets. They contained workshops, pet dealers, storage areas and cafes. Stalls lined Brick Lane and extended down to the Petticoat Lane clothing market. It offered everything for sale that anyone could want and was popular for the sale of animals. You could buy anything from a goldfish to illegal exotic pets. The area at that time, was, to put it mildly, rather seedy and there were many dodgy characters involved with the transactions.

Each Sunday, two RSPCA Inspectors patrolled the place, called in from all over London to take their turn at trying to contain the illegal trade in wild birds and monitor the welfare of the animals sold there. Club Row was a centre for the trade in illegally caught wild songbirds. The hobby of competing these birds to establish which had the best song, had been a tradition in the East End for hundreds of years, and was accompanied by betting on which was the best bird. This activity is still very popular all over South East Asia and other parts of the world. Prize birds were very valuable and the hobby attracted many unsavoury characters who insisted on illegally capturing wild birds. This involved setting up hides and nets to catch such birds as Redpolls, Greenfinches and Goldfinches. Nearby Hackney Marshes was still quite a wild place at the time and bird trapping occurred there, with the RSPCA Inspectors and Police catching trappers on a regular basis. Many birds died or got injured during the capture process and those that survived were offered for sale in the market. Furtive deals took place in the dingy, smoke laden pubs and cafes that lined the market.

Several of the arches housed the premises of animal dealers trading in all species of pets either legally or illegally. Outside in the street amongst the stalls there were private individuals selling puppies and kittens. These were the unwanted litters of unneutered pets, on which the owners hoped to make some extra pocket money. Others were illegal traders who bred the puppies and kittens purposefully and then stood and sold them from a box in the street. The local East End RSPCA Inspector at the time, whose patch the market was situated in, was a stocky ex-paratrooper named John who I thought was great as he wouldn't put up with any nonsense. On seeing someone selling puppies from a box his approach was usually:

'Are you selling those puppies?'

'No', the worried seller would reply as he knew he wasn't a licensed stall-holder, 'I'm trying to find good homes for them'.

'Well it's your lucky day. You have found good homes for the lot with me', and with that he would pick the box up and walk off. Any argument and John stood his ground. At the end of the morning I would drive down in the ambulance and collect all the puppies and kittens that the Inspectors had rounded up. I returned them to the hospital where they were checked over and given a good feed and if healthy they were transported to one of our animal homes the next day.

Unfortunately many members of the public bought puppies and kittens from the market either as a spur of the moment purchase, because they felt sorry for them, or because they ignorantly thought the market a good place to acquire a pet. The animals sold there were notoriously sickly individuals. The kittens suffered from flu and enteritis and the pups Distemper, worms, gastroenteritis and Leptospirosis. The new owners would troop into local RSPCA clinics a day or so later with these poor animals held in their arms. It was heart-breaking stuff to see the cute little things so miserable, with eye and nose discharges and uncontrollable diarrhoea. Most of them tragically died after a short fight for life and even if they survived many were left with side effects. Puppies developed an uncontrollable nervous twitch, a common side effect of Distemper. Many spent all the time vomiting and passing evil diarrhoea, getting thinner daily. If they died, the owners would sadly return to the market to get another one. It was a case of better luck next time, as they couldn't afford to acquire a pet from a more reputable place. The traders were quite happy about the situation as they made a lot of money out of this suffering.

The clinics kept a register of all puppies bought from the market and treated. These statistics were sent monthly to our Headquarters. They were then used as evidence to try and get the local Council to ban the sale of animals, but they were apparently unsympathetic, as even with many years of campaigning, this terrible trade continued with countless numbers of animals suffering and dying as a result. Thankfully Club Row market is now consigned to history.

*   *   *

'They're in there with the dustbins', said the little girl.

I was surrounded by a group of excited young kids who all wanted to be the one to show me where the kittens were. I had been called to a typical sixties block of flats on a depressing housing estate situated in Bethnal Green. The flats had a chute on each floor where residents threw their bags of rubbish down to big bins contained in a room at the bottom. Whilst playing in this undesirable area, they had heard pitiful meows and discovered some kittens. The children all tried to enter the door at the same time in their haste to show me.

'Give me some space please so that I can have a look. How about just one of you show me?' I pleaded, as the jostling group of tried to squeeze through the entrance doorway. They parted, and as I entered, the evil smell of rotting waste on a warm summer afternoon permeated my nostrils.

'They're in the bin there mate', said a little boy pointing.

I looked into the bin while the kids crowded round. There were four or five kittens, about three weeks old, squirming around amongst the rubbish. We were often called out to these situations, as residents, on occasions, would purposefully and callously dump, sick or unwanted animals down these chutes, sometimes tied in bags. In this case, it was difficult to know whether a mother cat had deposited them there herself or whether they were dumped. What was certain was that they were in a terrible state and suffering from Feline Upper Respiratory Disease or Cat Flu, as it is commonly called. It was rife in London due to the large stray cat population. Many unvaccinated owned cats, coming into contact with the strays, would come down with it. Kittens and aged cats are particularly susceptible and these kittens were in a real mess. As I lifted them out, one by one, I could see that their eyes were totally gummed up and swollen. Their noses were virtually blocked with mucous streaming out of their nostrils. Every now and again they would emit a little sneeze. There is no more miserable sight than a cat suffering from full-blown flu and my heart went out to them. Constant violent sneezing, high temperature and a discharge from the eyes and nose, are enough to make anyone miserable. A cat will sit there hunched up, having trouble breathing, dribbling saliva and reluctant to move, and in the worst cases, horrible ulcers develop on the tongue, making it painful to eat resulting in dehydration and weight loss.

The virus is highly infectious and airborne droplets pass it on when they sneeze. Giving antibiotic treatment and fluids by a drip will lead to recovery in many instances. Basic nursing can make them much happier and constant clearing of the nose, eyes and mouth with warm water and cotton wool can work wonders. With a blocked up nose, it cannot smell its food, so it is important to tempt the cat with something smelly like pilchards, and it may even be necessary to syringe or force-feed. Unfortunately, in some cases, the disease was too severe, and it was unfair to put them through the misery of a long drawn out death. Feral or wild cats are almost impossible to treat and many died. Those that do recover often build up immunity. In this case, the kittens were really past help as their eyes were virtually destroyed by the infection behind the swollen, caked mess.

'Are they going to be alright, Mister?' asked one of the kids.

Although I hate to lie to people, I couldn't bring myself to tell them that they were beyond help and that they would have to be put to sleep.

I'm going to take them back to see our vet who I'm sure will be able to do something'.

I thanked them profusely for reporting the plight of the kittens, as it is always good to promote animal welfare with young people at every opportunity. With that I put them in the back of the van and drove off.

*   *   *

On quiet, hot, summer Sunday afternoons, one of us often drove down to Camden Town, to the wonderful

Italian Marine ice cream parlour opposite the Roundhouse. After buying a large tub, I had to zoom back in the ambulance before it had a chance to melt. My colleague and the nurse, with bowls, would greet me at the reception door in hand and we would sit devouring it. On these occasions, it was a pleasurable habit to rescue an animal or two from the wards and let

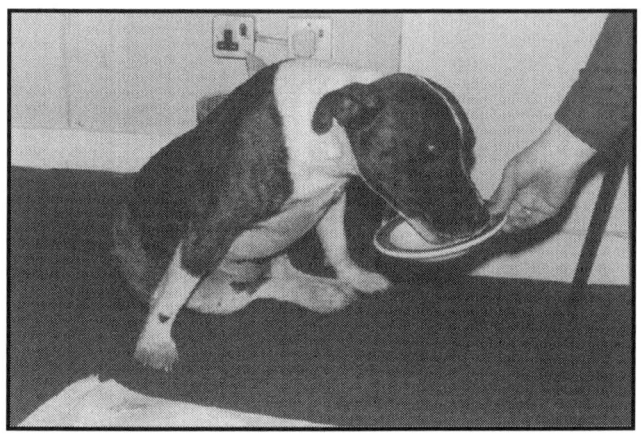

An injured dog would often join us and help finish off the ice cream.

them join us in reception. One of the great pleasures of working in an animal rescue establishment is that you have a constant supply of kittens and puppies to play with, and it was rather like an animal Peter Pan world. The trouble with owning young animals is that they grow up very quickly into an adult and the cute days are soon gone. With all the puppies and kittens passing through the hospital, either owned or stray, there was always some little mite to entertain and play with. There is nothing like watching puppies as they bounced sideways across the office floor in excitement, yapping their heads off, or giving little growls as they stalked your foot. An excited kitten chasing something across the floor with its back arched and fur flaring out is another great sight. We had great times with them, it passed the time for us, and I am sure it did the same for them. Often, a stray dog from the ward joined us, perhaps recovering from a broken leg, so that it got out of its cage for a while. The dog would sit there with a huge support bandage wrapped round its leg and shared our ice cream, which was always gratefully received.

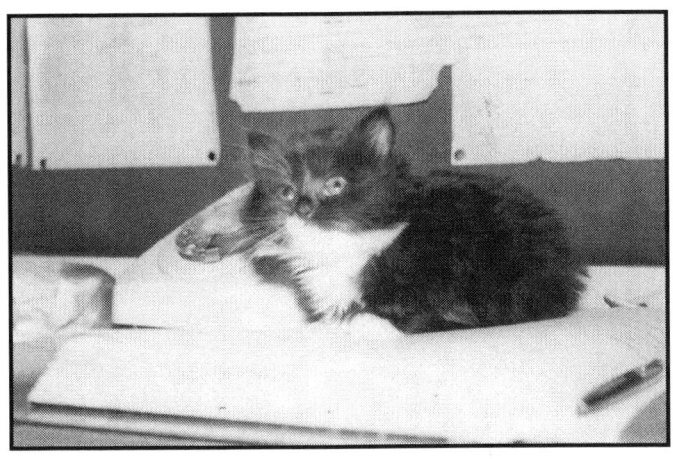

A stray kitten helps answer the emergency telephone

*   *   *

I pulled up outside Euston Station and parked in a restricted zone hoping that my RSPCA Emergency sign would dissuade any traffic warden or similar official from giving me a ticket. I walked into the concourse, looked up at the signage above and followed the arrow to the left luggage lockers. Being Sunday there were few passengers and even the tannoy announcements were few and far between. This was good news, as I needed a bit of quiet for the task I now had to perform. Someone had heard what they thought were the meows of a cat coming from the area of the left luggage lockers and I needed to listen. Having found the long tiered row of small lockers I stood close to them, cocked my head and listened. Nothing that sounded like a cat came to my ears. I changed position several times and listened again to no avail and I was beginning to think that this was a hoax call or the caller had perhaps heard a child playing around. I started tapping them to see if this caused any response and to my surprise, I suddenly heard a faint meowing sound. Surely, some idiot had not put a cat into one of them? As I looked round for inspiration, I saw a uniformed railwayman approaching me with a young woman in tow.

'Hi there. Are you the RSPCA? I didn't think we had telephoned you yet,' he said.

'Well actually someone else called us about hearing a cat here and I was checking it out,' I replied.

'I'm from the left luggage section and this lady has reported the same thing. Have you heard it?' he asked.

'I have, just a second ago,' I informed him.

'Where exactly is the noise coming from?'

'I'm not sure, but when I tapped them I think I heard it meowing.'

'Let's give it another go shall we,' the railwayman suggested.

The three of us leaned closely towards the lockers and I gave another tap. Sure enough, we all heard the sound.

'There is definitely a cat inside one of these lockers!' he exclaimed astounded.

'I think you are right,' I agreed.

'I'll go and get some reinforcements and we'll investigate.'

'I'll go and get a basket and meet you back here,' I said.

Five minutes later all of us were tapping the doors until we finally pinpointed which one the sound was emanating from.

'If you get ready, Mr RSPCA man, I'll get my colleague here to open the door and you can see what is inside and get hold of it if necessary.'

I stood next to him with my basket and he opened the door. For a second we both had to lean back because of the awful smell that exploded out, caused by the poor cat messing itself. Large eyes blinked at the daylight and a slightly bewildered friendly little black and white female cat leaned forward to greet us. I quickly grabbed her and put her into the basket in case she tried to escape, but she was too relieved to see us and just wanted some attention.

'Poor thing, I wonder what idiot put her in there. It's lucky the door isn't airtight,' said the shocked man from left luggage.

'It's terrible,' I agreed, 'can you let us know if anyone enquires about her. I will inform one of our Inspectors as they will definitely want to speak to the owner.'

'I certainly will.'

'Thank you and I don't fancy being the person who has to clean that out,' I said.

On the journey back, I too had to suffer the smell wafting from the back, but she was soon cleaned, fed and checked over and did not seem to have suffered from her ordeal. It turned out that she had been in the locker for twelve hours. Her owner did turn up later and her lame excuse was that the cat was only supposed to be in the locker for an hour or two, but she had been admitted into hospital overnight and couldn't get back.

*   *   *

Birds as big as pigeons, for some reason, had a habit of falling down chimneys. They love to perch on the stacks and pots and perhaps a gust of wind might catch them off balance blowing them in or a bad landing might result in the bird toppling in, but it was difficult to surmise how they managed it. Once in, they were unable to fly out due to the confined space, and when flapping their wings to try to escape, only fell further down to find themselves well and truly trapped and facing a lonely, dark, slow death from starvation.

In 2012, the skeleton of a pigeon was discovered in the chimney of an old house in Surrey undergoing renovation. Strapped to the skeletal leg was a capsule containing a coded message revealing that the messenger pigeon had flown across the channel from occupied France in 1941 and had fallen in and died. It had taken 70 years for the little hero's exploits to be revealed, and shows that pigeons have been falling down chimneys for a very long time. Far more people in those days had open fires or gas fires blocking the hearth and very few had any form of ventilated covering over the top to stop birds falling in.

The birds rarely dropped straight down as the design of the old chimneys involved a series of ledges on which the birds perched on their journey down. They would sit there during the daylight hours continually attempting to fly up towards the light and exhausting themselves in the process. The homeowner would then find or hear debris falling down. Probably from loneliness or despair, the birds often called out and the plaintive cries were magnified. If the house had a gas fire fitted, the fireplace was usually sealed off, so that when the bird eventually found itself at the bottom, there was no escape. Constant scrambling behind the fire would alert the householders that something was there resulting in an urgent telephone call for our assistance.

Rescuing them could take a few minutes to a couple of days depending on the circumstances. The easiest rescue was when a bird had fallen straight down into the open. By the time I arrived, the bird was flying round the room and I would find a hysterical person standing amongst clouds of soot. It was then just a case of entering to retrieve it. If it was still perched half way up the chimney, then it was far more difficult. A bird's natural instinct is to try to fly up and out of trouble, particularly when they can see light at the end of the tunnel or in this case the chimney. Poking rods up often knocked them down along with a mass of black soot and debris, but more often than not, this did not have the desired effect.

Another trick was to try to convince the bird that down was up. Placing a torch or table lamp at the bottom and either drawing the curtains to darken the room or leaving it overnight often convinced it to head down towards the light of the lamp. Going down was much easier than trying to fly up. Of course, the owner of the house usually had a terrible mess in the morning if it did appear, but this happened whichever method we used.

When they were stuck behind a gas fire or a bricked up fireplace the real fun began. We had an agreement with the Gas Board that one of their engineers would attend free of charge when we had confirmed that a bird required rescuing and was in distress. Once I had done this, the engineer would normally arrive very quickly, so I would wait around if possible so that I was there to check the bird over and take it away. The worst scenario was when a bird was trapped behind a bricked or boarded up fireplace. Then a major decision had to be made, as the rescue could involve damage to the property and result in a large bill for repairs that the house owner might expect us to pay. This kind of situation always sorted out the true compassionate person from the pseudo animal lover.

I can only remember one occasion when I had to call out a building contractor to remove a bricked and boarded up fireplace. It was agreed that the Society paid for the initial removal work, but not for making good and decorating after the rescue. As often happens, the builder was so keen to rescue the "poor mite" that he didn't bother to charge us anything.

*   *   *

The last emergency surgery of the weekend began at seven o'clock on a Sunday evening and it tended to be a busy one. Some forty-eight hours had passed since most private vets had operated a normal service, or had been contactable, and their clients would be turning up stating they couldn't afford the fees they had been quoted, or they couldn't get hold of the vet at all. Some of our own clients, who we had been trying to deal with by giving first aid advice over the telephone, would now start arriving. The measures we had advised had not improved the condition of their pets, so we would relent and ask them in. Owners filed in with dogs and cats suffering from infectious diseases; a limping or coughing dog, or perhaps a road accident cat. The variety of injuries and illnesses presented at the emergency surgeries was endless.

Late Sunday evening was a time when we started to feel shattered. Nearly thirty-six hours had passed since we had started our shift. The last evening surgery was over, but we still had another night of telephone calls and possible call outs to get through before we could finally leave the hospital. It was quite a responsibility to deal with these calls late at night, once the safety net of the vet and nurse had departed. Most of the enquiries we received during the night were from owners who required reassurance that their sick pet would be safe to leave until the morning for treatment. This immediately put the onus and responsibility onto us, which was always a worry, as making a judgement on an animal we did not know or could not see was difficult. Many owners telephoned us as they did not want "to disturb their own vet at this time of night!" This always went down well with us.

The advice and decisions we made could mean life or death for the animal concerned. We were not qualified veterinary surgeons or even qualified nurses, but were asked to make decisions on behalf of the duty vets to save them from being permanently present at the hospital. It was the same with owners arriving unannounced at the door with their ailing pet. With experience though, came confidence, and I found it was possible to deal with most situations without giving it a thought. It was important to establish if their pet was suffering from a life threatening condition that required immediate treatment and luckily, there are only a few of these so it was easy to remember them.

Top of the list was the gastric torsion: a very painful and quickly deteriorating condition where the stomach literally flips over blocking both ends. The stomach swells with gas to an alarming size and if left untreated ruptures and the dog dies very quickly. Then there was the infected womb or pyometra in an unspayed female. There are two types, but in both cases the womb fills with pus and either type is life threatening. Another condition I kept in mind was eclampsia: where a nursing mother is sucked dry of calcium reducing the dog to fits, convulsions and collapse.

Apart from these dire emergencies, there were stock answers to many of the ailments that owners telephoned about. A vomiting pet or one that had bloodless diarrhoea was advised to be starved for 24 hours and then offered small amounts of boiled water to drink, followed by a little boiled white fish, chicken and rice for a further 24 hours. Nine times out of ten the animal was probably just suffering from an upset stomach and like humans this regime of care was the best course of action. Even these basic ailments were problematic, as an animal that was vomiting, but was not going to the toilet, might have had an intestinal obstruction, which might be serious. We always advised telephoning back if the animal deteriorated. If it was a kitten or puppy then it was a different matter as they can go downhill very quickly. If animals were passing blood in the vomit or diarrhoea, then again, it was more serious and owners were told to bring the animal in to the next emergency surgery.

Dogs with coughs could be given Benylin or a similar human cough medicine and then allowed small amounts of water to drink so as not to irritate the sore throat. Cats with suspected abscesses could have a poultice applied and animals that were not eating had to be tempted with smelly fish such as pilchards or sardines, plus Brands Essence, a concentrated food tonic. Thus it went on.

First aid advice that we gave over the telephone was very limited as we could never be quite certain what the problem was, and whether advising the owner to do something might make it worse. In most cases it was obvious whether it required immediate attention. Obviously if a wound was bleeding badly then advising a tourniquet or tight bandage could do no harm. Cases of poisoning were common either from chewing on a poisoned rat or mouse carcass or lapping up some antifreeze which unbelievably dogs find has a very sweet taste. Puppies had a habit of licking lead based paint, which was in general use in those days. Giving washing soda crystals, salt water and hydrogen peroxide induces vomiting which sometimes can help. An old vet once told me that a mixture of milk of magnesia, burnt toast and strong tea was a universal remedy to help neutralize a variety of poisons. With far more open fires around then, dogs and cats often suffered burns or scalds from embers falling out of the grate as they stretched out in front of the fire. In these cases immediate dousing with cold water was the best first aid.

Last thing at night, before locking up and retiring to the night room, we always checked the front of the hospital. Although we had a security camera, it was a very poor quality affair and was next to useless. On occasions, people crept up to the hospital after dark and left a box of puppies or kittens in the shadows somewhere, or dumped an adult cat in a flimsy box, with a note attached, along the lines of "please look after Tibby, as we cannot". Often by the time we found the box the cat had clawed its way out and escaped. It was not unknown for a dog to be tied up outside. It used to annoy me immensely as these owners had made the effort to come all the way to the hospital and by doing so must have had some feelings for the animal, but then irresponsibly abandoned them. The worst consequence of leaving adult animals in this way was that we often couldn't establish the name, age, and other history, which was a shame.

On a Sunday night we tried to get our heads down at midnight which was quite early and took a chance on being disturbed soon after bedding down. It was rare not to get a telephone call or someone turning up unannounced at the door during the night and there was always another road accident, rescue or fire to attend to.

*   *   *

'A driver saw him along here somewhere, mate,' said the train driver.

This was the first of only two occasions when I got to travel up front with the driver of a Tube train. It was a bit of a squash, as an Underground manager and a Transport Policeman accompanied me. We were not actually underground, but travelling along one of the over ground sections in the East End. Several drivers and passengers had reported seeing a dog curled up beside the track and I had been asked to investigate. As the dog had been sighted half way between stations it had been decided not to walk, partly because of the distance, but also because it was beginning to get dark. I am sure we were breaking all sorts of regulations. As the train trundled along at a slow speed we all gazed at the right hand side of the track where everyone had noticed the dog.

'There it is,' shouted the Policeman, pointing ahead.

We followed the line of his outstretched hand and about fifty feet ahead we could make out a black shape on the edge of the long grass. The train came to a screeching halt. I was assured that all trains had been stopped at red lights in both directions, while we searched for the dog. There must have been a lot of unhappy commuters at this moment. We climbed down with difficulty, as without a platform, it was surprising how much of a drop it was. I was armed with a grasper, a lead and a first aid box, as I always like to be prepared. In cases like this, you cannot nip back to the van to get something.

I asked the others to stay back and I tentatively approached the small dog, half expecting it to raise its head and immediately exit stage left. As I crunched over the ballast, he made no movement at all and my next concern was that he was dead. I crouched down beside him and he suddenly started shivering so I knew he was alive. I spoke quietly, as you do in these circumstances, something along the lines of "what's happened to you then?" or "how are you my old mate": anything to make first contact and put the animal at ease. He made the effort to raise his head and look at me and the shivering became more violent. He was the cutest black and white puppy, about four months old, with wonderfully long ears and a white strip running down between his appealing eyes. I gingerly put my hand towards him expecting a nip, but his little tail started to make a half-hearted wag. Emboldened by this I stroked him on the head and he started to whimper. He then rolled on his side and I suddenly noticed that one of his front legs was missing, just above the elbow, probably severed by the wheel of a train and there was just a bloody stump with the bone protruding. Although in the past I had dealt with many mangled animals, I have to admit that at this point, I was quite upset at the sight. Here was this cute little puppy, all alone and seriously injured, lying by the track in the dark and cold, with no expectation of help or rescue. He had obviously resigned himself to his fate and had curled up to die. This would certainly have been the result if he had crawled further into the grass and not been spotted. Animals have such fortitude, as unlike humans, they do not have the same thought process and knowledge to know that they can expect aid from an ambulance crew, treatment at a hospital and be told of their chances of recovery.

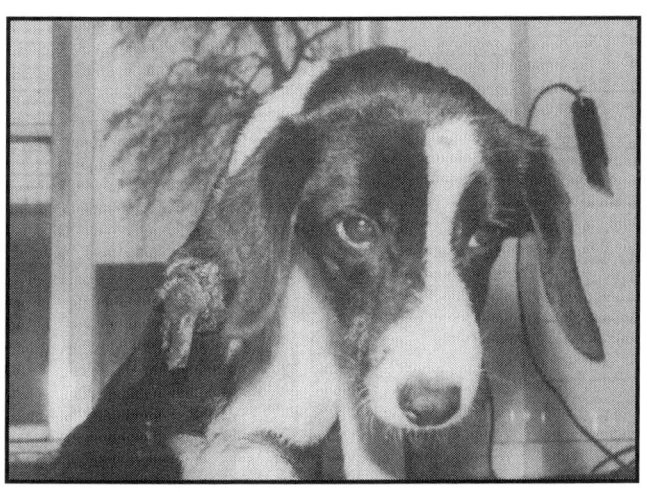

I suddenly noticed one of his front legs was missing

He was more than willing for me to lift him up, still shivering, keen on human contact and help. My two companions gathered around and, like me, were saddened at his plight. Here we were, three grown men, beside a railway track in the dark making silly sounds of compassion to a shocked and depressed little dog.

'We'll get him back in the train and go on to the next station. I'll radio ahead and get transport for you back to your van,' offered the Policeman.

'That sounds great,' I accepted.

He got back in the train and I gently passed the puppy up to him. He was quite keen to cradle him in his arms to the next stop where we alighted and walked through the station. Passengers on the platform gave concerned looks as we passed by. After a few minutes a police car arrived and took us back to our starting point. I placed the puppy on the front seat next to me wrapped in a thick blanket.

Next day the rest of the leg was amputated and he survived his ordeal and proved to be a delightful pup who quickly found a home. Animals soon adapt to having only three legs and after practice can tear around like any four-legged dog. Although it has been over forty years since I rescued that puppy, I have never forgotten his little face and stoic bravery.

*   *   *

When the day staff arrived early on Monday morning they would be met by a couple of zombies looking like death warmed up. We sat hunched over a cup of tea or coffee, grunted at arriving staff and waited for the clock to tick round to our knocking off time. Finally it was time to go and we would stagger into the night room, get changed and wander out the front door to return to the outside world. Another weekend shift was over and, although tired out, I would be quite elated as I had three days off before having to return.

5:

Swanning About on the River

The mighty River Thames formed the southern boundary of our area and we were responsible for any incidents on the river, from Westminster Bridge by the Houses of Parliament to Silvertown and North Woolwich. For someone who loved boats and water, this was heaven sent and I looked forward to any chance to spend time on or near the river. Luckily this was quite often.

Many of the old docks were still in use, although their demise was not far off. I loved any opportunity to wander along the few remaining wharves staring up at the large ships tethered by ropes the circumference of a telegraph pole. The docks were a hive of activity with derricks offloading the cargo and huge containers. The Dockers were a breed apart, always moaning and swearing, but would drop everything in order to help me in the rescue of an animal. Many of the old warehouses were still in use and provided an atmosphere, which is now long gone. The dock areas are now very sanitized, the buildings replaced with offices, the warehouses turned into expensive apartments and the large ships replaced by yachts in marinas. I have always been thankful that I was able to experience some of the excitement of the docks before they disappeared.

The King George V dock was one that was still operating and on one occasion I was called to catch a swan that had crashed landed by the entrance gate.

When I arrived I found a long traffic jam trying to enter and a large male swan standing in the middle of the road keeping everyone at bay. The security staff were making valiant efforts to move it out of the way, but it was resisting all their efforts. The poor thing was obviously very disorientated and angry and would have none of it. With his wings flapping, he ran at them hissing and forcing them to retreat. There is something wonderful about being confronted by a huge male swan, rearing up to its full height, hissing and flapping its wings. It is a fearsome sight, but having faced such scenarios many times before the aggression did not have an effect on me. They have a reputation for being able to cause injury to humans by breaking an arm with the leading edge of their wings. Although I treated them with great respect, I knew that the display was more of a bluff. I nonchalantly walked up to him, lunged forward, grabbed him round the neck and quickly sat on him, much to the amazement of all the assembled spectators. It was a great feeling when a capture went to plan and impressed in that way. I have to admit that the first time I had to catch hold of a swan had been a very frightening experience, but it soon became second nature.

The trick to subduing one was to get hold of the wings. If you controlled the wings the bird normally became very passive. The swan hook was a useful piece of equipment for catching them, although I normally only used it when they were on water. Shaped like a shepherd's crook on the end of a pole, it allowed you to grab them round the neck from a distance. I preferred the direct approach of rushing in and grabbing the neck with my hands. Once I had a hold, it was a case of concentrating on the wings. Getting a knee gently on the swan's back or half-sitting astride it are good methods. Then I gathered the wings in and folded them into place and I had caught my swan. Once subdued it was normally quite happy to have its legs and body enclosed in a bag or sack and to be transported in the back of the van. In fact, they made me smile as I watched them in the rear view mirror, sitting in the back with their heads held high, obviously taking great interest in the passing world outside the window.

Swans were our most regular customers on the Thames. The river supported a huge population of them. Great flotillas could be seen gliding along or preening themselves on the mud banks at low tide. I have a soft spot for them as they are one of my favourite birds and it was such a pleasure to help them. They do no harm to anyone unless disturbed. They are intelligent and elegant birds with attributes that humans could learn from. They pair for life and aggressively protect their young. They are quite successful at rearing most of their brood, which can number anything up to eight and it is such a pleasant sight to see a family flotilla gliding down a stream or pond. However they are particularly difficult to handle when protecting a nest during breeding season. If one partner was injured or sick and we were called to attend to it, I often had to fend the other away, as it would protect its sick mate; so it was best to capture both and following treatment release them together. If this was not possible I had to return the recovered sick or injured bird back to its partner as soon as possible.

The swans seen adorning the rivers and lakes of London are Mute swans. Originally wild birds of the Steppe lakes of Central Asia, they are now relatively tame birds, which enjoy being fed in local parks. They are very beautiful when they decide to gracefully curve their necks and arch their wings as they swim along. They are not quite as graceful when they take off as they are heavy birds and tend to noisily patter along the water surface with their big feet before taking off. They spend most of their time swimming and feed by extending their long necks below water, or if the water is deep, they upend to reach the lake or river bed.

Unfortunately, living on the Thames is not the easiest or safest habitat for them and they were always getting themselves into trouble, often through no fault of their own. Calls to swans in distress were a weekly occurrence, particularly in the spring and summer. Many of the dock areas, warehouses and railway yards had already closed down, but had been left derelict. They remained in limbo awaiting redevelopment, as vast swathes of waste ground littered with broken glass, wooden pallets, crates, rusting machinery and overgrown railway tracks. Buildings were vandalised and falling apart with windows smashed. These areas became havens for wildlife and stray animals. Swans sometimes crash landed, attracted probably by pools of water or perhaps by the greenery that was sprouting up. Once down they couldn't take off again or they cut their feet on the glass or got tangled up in barbed wire. Catching one on land was much easier than when they were on water, so this was not usually a problem for us. Oil spills though were a major problem.

On the odd occasion when there was a major oil spill affecting large groups of swans a rescue had to be organised. Such operations were never feasible without the co-operation of the River Police. In fact, it was usually them who alerted us and asked for our assistance. The River Police were the eyes and ears of the river and on their constant patrols were usually the first to notice any animal in distress. Historically, their main job was to counter smuggling and to make sure the laws of navigation were adhered to. They also had the unenviable task of retrieving dead human bodies. With the docks gradually closing and river traffic reducing, their job was already changing. Many of the officers had been navigating the river for years and knew every hazard, mud bank and every yard of embankment. They were a great bunch to spend time with.

One day in late summer they contacted us to report a group of swans, all with oil on them and wanted our assistance. We arranged a rescue operation for the following day, when three of us, including the local RSPCA Inspector, in two vans, headed to Wapping. The Police Station was situated beside the river in Wapping High Street and was like no other in London at the time. There were no shopping precincts here, just a narrow cobbled street lined with old warehouses and buildings. This was a really historic part of London, which had not changed since Victorian days. The Police Station even had an old blue lamp outside which conjured up visions of old 1930's films. I had been down there late at night when it was completely deserted and it was an extremely atmospheric and eerie place, giving an aura of Jack the Ripper days. It has totally changed now and is a more residential area, with a riverside park and countless apartments. From the front exterior, the Police Station looked like any other, but when you walked out the back door, instead of a yard full of police vehicles, you found a wide expanse of river. Several pontoons stretched out onto the water with police launches moored against them.

It was a bright warm sunny afternoon, the tide was low and calm and everything was perfect for swanning about on the river. Everyone was in high spirits, particularly the crew, who welcomed these operations as a pleasant change to their normal routine. We had a cup of tea while we waited for them to make final arrangements to cast off. Two boats had been assigned and our equipment was loaded on board. We headed eastwards down the river and we were informed that the swans were about a mile away. We motored round the great curve of Limehouse Reach and passed the India Docks. Our skipper was an old hand and in a jovial mood. He was pointing out the sights and regaling us with tales of strange and macabre events they had dealt with at different points along the river. We passed lines of barges being towed along and the occasional tourist boat full of sightseers listening to a commentary on the history of the river. We were getting our own conducted tour with far more bizarre stories and all for free. The skipper pointed ahead to a group of swans close to some moored barges. Several of them were stained black and one was particularly bad. We slowed as we approached them and the other boat came alongside.

'What's the plan of campaign then?' asked the other skipper.

'I think the best way is to try and get some of them between the boats and we will try and get a couple as they swim between us,' suggested our Inspector.

'We'll give it a try, but they are quick devils and can easily out manoeuvre us,' he replied without conviction.

He was quite right with this statement, as catching swans and ducks on large expanses of water is notoriously difficult and can take hours of perseverance. They have an amazing turn of speed when required. They are extremely intelligent and can normally second guess your intentions and will suddenly veer away to avoid capture. As a last resort to escape, they will fly off, if able to, a definite unfair advantage.

We steered straight for them, the launches about thirty feet apart. There were two of us on one launch and one on the other. We had attached our swan hooks to extension poles making them about ten feet long, but at that length, they become very cumbersome and heavy. As we neared, the swans' legs began to tread water at a fantastic pace and they started to disperse. One was not quite quick enough and my colleague Bob managed to get the hook round its neck, which resulted in a lot of loud snorting and thrashing of wings. The swan was hauled to the side of the launch and I was able to lean over and pull him up and into the launch getting soaked in the process. He thrashed about in the well of the boat for a while until a policeman and I got his wings under control and managed to put the bird's body and legs in a sack. Specially designed restraint bags are now available for this task that slip over the body and feet. The swan is strapped in and it even has carrying handles. Back then, though we had to suffice with good old Hessian sacks with the end tied round the swan's neck with bandage. Finding itself totally constrained, it gave a few more disgruntled snorts and then settled to watch our activities with interest. By this time, the other launch was chasing a single swan towards some barges and I could see Bob kneeling precariously at the bow with swan hook outstretched.

'Reminds me of one of your chaps a few years ago,' remarked the skipper suddenly 'he was a right know it all, ordering us all over the place and getting up our noses. He was in a similar situation to your mate over there, standing on the bow acting like Nelson. I was so fed up with him that I sailed the bow of the boat into a mud bank and pitched him off headfirst: purely by accident of course.'

We all laughed at this and I turned to watch in case the same fate occurred to Bob, but I saw the swan swim between two barges and my colleague bravely and athletically jumped on to one. He then ran along the side of the barge and managed to hook the swan and we had two in the bag. There were only another dozen or so to go. They regrouped about fifty yards away and we tried to herd them back towards the barges, hoping we could corral the swans between them. They refused to cooperate and the leader of the flotilla led them into the middle of the river. As time was getting on, we decided to concentrate on the most badly oiled ones. It took us a further three hours to catch four more and as the light was fading, we decided to call a halt to proceedings. We had captured the worst affected and believed the others would survive without cleaning. The police promised to keep an eye on them and inform us if they got worse. The six we had caught were lying together in the bottom of the launch, their necks entwined, giving them the look of a mythical creature with heads looking in all directions.

As we headed back to base at Wapping, the light faded fast and it became very cold. We all felt exhausted as it had been a very long afternoon and evening. The skipper spotted a disco boat cruising along without navigation lights.

'We'll cruise over and remind the captain,' he said.

He steered our launch alongside and he hailed the boat. A man appeared at the rail wearing a white coat.

'Tell the captain to switch his lights on,' he shouted across.

The man was obviously foreign with little grasp of English so he was shouted at again. He stared for a while and then disappeared.

'I don't think he understood,' said the skipper.

We followed alongside for a few seconds and then the man in the white coat appeared again carrying a crate of beer, which he gestured towards us. This caused a lot of laughter and the police told him off for attempted bribery. Eventually, another member of the crew appeared and the matter of the lights was settled. It was a great end to the day. The swans were loaded up in our vans and transported to the hospital for cleaning. They all recovered and eventually they were united with their friends, none the worse for their experience.

*   *   *

Oiling of swans and other birds can cause a lot of misery. When a bird is covered in oil, it stops the feathers from meshing together properly and so the water can penetrate, the bird becomes waterlogged and can easily sink and drown. If there is a large amount on the bird, it cannot cope with cleaning itself and by trying to do so will swallow the toxic oil. The combination of the two, results in them suffering from a variety of symptoms. Ingesting causes inflammation and burning of the gut and other internal organs. This leads to enteritis, starvation and ultimately death.

If the bird is not badly soiled and hasn't swallowed much then it only requires bathing. This is ascertained by checking if the bird has a lot of oil in its mouth and if it is passing oil when it goes to the toilet. To clean a swan a large sink, bath or container was filled with a one percent solution of washing up liquid in warm water. The bird was put in the bath up to its neck and held for a while followed by gentle rubbing and parting the feathers so that the liquid penetrated right into the plumage. The head has to be carefully washed with a sponge or small brush. It was back breaking work and took a long time to clean even a slightly oiled one, as we had to keep putting it in a new clean solution and repeating the process. Finally, the bird had to be rinsed off with warm water. All this cleaning removed the waterproofing qualities of the feathers, so they were kept for a while before being released, otherwise they could sink and drown when attempting to swim.

Swans can have a tough time trying to survive and enjoy life in urban London. Although they have a plentiful supply of water and habitat in the form of rivers, canals, lakes and reservoirs, interaction with humans was always their downfall. Anglers were one of their main enemies and I lost count of how many times I had to capture and collect swans with lead poisoning or with hooks and line caught in their beaks and gullets. In those unenlightened times lead fishing weights the size of small peas were in general use, which had a slit in them through which the line was passed and squeezed shut. An angler would have hundreds of them in a tin and often they were deliberately or accidentally discarded on the bank of the canal or lake.

Often a line would snag on something and break and the lead weights would sink to the bottom. Swans andducks, which mainly graze the waterbed, would then pick up the hook and line or be attracted to the small round beads on the bank thinking them food to eat. The lead collects in the gizzard and some can have dozens of pellets lodged there, but it does not take much to start poisoning them. The lead is continuously absorbed during the digestion process and the level builds up until the bird becomes ill. The obvious sign of lead poisoning was usually a bird lying on the bank looking weak, thin and anaemic and even showing signs of nerve damage and paralysis. The neck becomes

Swans can have a tough time surviving in London.

paralysed and it was a sad and pathetic sight to find a once beautiful swan reduced to being unable to raise its head and neck. We had many dead ones reported to us and even those that were alive when I collected them often died despite treatment. I rushed them back to the hospital and a quick x-ray would confirm if there were lead pellets in the gizzard. The only chance of recovery was to control the diarrhoea with antibiotics and a

Kaolin mixture and try to get food into the sick bird. It was a very miserable experience for the swans and it took many days for them to recover. There was considerable publicity about the situation and, following pressure, the angling industry did become organized and lead weights were mostly replaced with non-toxic material. Unfortunately, it took a very long time and many swans died horrible deaths in the process.

* * *

'There it is mate: the one nearest to us lying down,' pointed out one of a group of concerned Dockers.

I had received a call earlier from them, as they were worried about a swan on a mud bank below the wharf they were working on, that had not moved for several hours. Like the River Police, it was pleasing to know that these men had the compassion to worry over an animal in distress and report it. Now that the scene along the river has changed, I wonder how many sick animals go unnoticed. There were six swans on the exposed mud bank and the one in question had its head tucked under one wing and wasn't moving.

'It hasn't moved all morning and we're afraid it will drown when the tide comes in,' he added.

I had brought Gordon, a colleague along, as this kind of rescue can be difficult without help. I pointed out that it could be just sleeping, but I knew there was something wrong with it and we would have to attempt a rescue.

'Is the mud very deep?' I asked, hoping the answer was no.

'Nah, you'll only sink a little bit,' he assured us.

'I'll take your word for it,' I said, unconvinced.

Wearing waders and carrying a swan hook, my colleague and I descended the vertical iron ladder down to the mud. The first couple of yards we traversed were very firm underfoot and we were filled with confidence. Five of the swans wandered away and kept their distance, giving us the occasional warning snort. The one we were after didn't even bother to look up at their departure, which was a worrying sign. Gordon started to stride towards the incumbent swan and suddenly disappeared up to his knees in the mud. I couldn't stop laughing as he was well and truly stuck. I edged close to him and reached over with my hand, but pulling him free was a nightmare as the suction was so great. Eventually he made it to firmer ground, but the smell he had stirred up was overpowering. Anyone who has had dealings with the Thames mud will know the smell.

'I think we have a problem,' Gordon declared.

I climbed back up the ladder, but the Dockers had returned to work and were unavailable to help. I looked around and spied a pile of wooden planks not far away. On closer inspection, there were only three that were serviceable.

'I think I have a solution,' I shouted down.

I dragged the three planks over to the edge of the wharf and let them drop to the mud below then climbed down after them.

'We'll use these to walk out to the swan,' I said.

'This should be a laugh.'

The planks were quite heavy, but we got one on end and let it drop onto the mud. Grabbing the second by both ends we walked along the first plank and repeated the procedure. It was definitely easier said than done as our boots were covered in the evil smelling, slimy substance which made the first plank slippery in no time. As we wavered precariously back and forth with the third plank, I wondered what would happen if we fell in as there was no one watching who could rescue us. The third plank went down and we were now exhausted and plastered head to foot. We were still some six feet short and I realised we would have to lift the first plank and carry it to the front, thus cutting off our return. Retrieving it turned into a major problem, as we had pushed it into the mud with our weight and the suction was so great we couldn't budge it. We finally lifted it, almost falling in again in the process and by plonking it back by the third plank we reached the swan, which had not reacted to all the noise and activity of our approach. I stepped forward and knelt down, the swan still didn't move and I thought that after all our efforts it might be dead. I gently removed her head from under her wing and could see she was still alive, but only just. The third eyelids were flickering across dull eyes and she didn't have the strength to keep her head up. I gently lifted the bird and she made no attempt to struggle.

Having tucked the swan under my arm, I followed Gordon to the end of our slippery impromptu walkway. It then dawned on us that we would have to retrieve the end plank and place it so we could get back to firm ground. Gordon was in front of me so I had to pass the swan to him to hold while I tried to retrieve the plank. This time I lost my balance and one leg went into the mud almost up to my thigh so that I was now half sitting. We were both in hysterics and almost crying. Gordon tucked the prone swan under his arm and used his free hand to try to pull me out. Again the suction was terrific and the smell awful. It took a while, but eventually I was free. I struggled to move the plank and then passed it to my colleague who gave me the swan. He dropped the plank and we were back on firm ground again.

We were so exhausted and our waders and hands were covered in so much slime that we were unable to climb back up the ladder. A nearby crane operator saw our predicament and helpfully lowered a pallet right by our side. We clambered on and clung to the chains supporting the pallet. We were lifted up on to the quay and, waving thanks to the crane operator, we headed for the van laying the limp bird in the back. We thankfully removed our waders and walked over to the Dockers and informed them that the outlook was not good. They thanked us for all our efforts and we headed back leaving the planks in situ. We couldn't face rescuing them. Unfortunately the swan did not recover and died during the night despite treatment. It was believed she had been poisoned.

* * *

Swans and ducks that had picked up hooks fared better as, once caught, they could be anaesthetised and operated on to remove the hook and line from wherever it was lodged. The problem here was catching them in the first place. Most of them were quite healthy and lively and had to be chased and cornered on park lakes and canals by using boats. This could take hours of patient mind games. The birds were not aware that we were trying to help them.

In the early seventies, we also had a spate of ducks and gulls contracting botulism. This is a toxin of a bacterium, which grows on the vegetation in shallow parts of lakes or stagnant water, particularly in hot weather. The poor birds absorb the organism when they eat the vegetable matter, small aquatic bugs or fly larvae. It is a strong poison and paralyses the legs, wings and neck. When I picked up a bird suffering from botulism, the neck and head would flop over, liquid seeped from their nose and beak and they had glazed half closed eyes. They were a pathetic and sorry sight and it was tragic that little could be done to save them. The outbreak killed many and I was kept very busy responding to reports of sick birds.

Swans were not the only animals getting into trouble along the river. Some maintenance workers carrying out repair work on Tower Bridge spotted a small animal trying to fight against the tide below them, as it was dragged along the river. On closer inspection, they discovered it was a deer and gave us a frantic telephone call. In these situations, there is little I could do as it takes quite a long time to reach the scene, but the workers had the common sense to hail a passing boat, which rescued the deer and brought it to the shore. When I arrived, the workers had it in their shed. The deer had been so cold, exhausted and shocked that it just lay there under a pile of rags quivering. It turned out to be a delightful little Muntjac deer. These are tiny delicate creatures, which are not native to the country, but were introduced and escaped. They are now thriving and wander the parks, railway embankments and back gardens of London.

They are solitary creatures and shy, so are rarely seen, but we would often get calls when they were hit by cars or got themselves trapped. This one had a long bleeding gash down the side of its muzzle. The poor thing was very frightened, its eyes wild, so I had to be careful. They can get into such a panic when approached that they will throw themselves into walls or fences and do themselves more damage. Catching a deer in the open is a case of being as quiet as possible, using slow movements until the last moment when you leap on the creature or catch it in a net. Once in captivity they suffer a lot of stress and any strange noise or human presence can set them off in a panic. This particular deer was shocked and exhausted, so was relatively calm and I was able to scoop him up in a blanket without too much fuss. Getting them into darkness such as a blanket over their head or into a darkened cage or box calms them immediately. Back at the hospital, his wound was treated and he was placed in a dark, quiet cage to warm up and relax. He was later removed to a wildlife unit in the countryside and eventually released.

Dogs were always falling or jumping into the Thames often closely followed by their owners or concerned onlookers. Jumping in to save your beloved pet is obviously instinctive and I would probably do the same if it was mine, but nine times out of ten, it is a futile exercise. Most dogs are natural swimmers and they have a powerful self-survival instinct and will usually make it back to safety whereas the rescuer can be swept away or drown.

Whenever I got a report of a dog in the river, I did not particularly rush to the scene as it was usually rescued by some kind-hearted soul long before I got there. I remember attending a call to a dog reported floundering in the River Lee at Plaistow, only to find a very cold and sodden police officer on the bank. He had been passing and a group of labourers had pointed the dog out to him. In a fit of bravado, he had immediately jumped in and pulled the animal to the bank where the labourers grabbed hold and took it to their shed. When I arrived, the dog was being rubbed down with cloths while the police officer tried to get a lift home. A similar incident occurred on a canal in Hackney where the owner of a barge jumped in and rescued a dog before I arrived and I found the two of them steaming in front of a fire on the barge.

*   *   *

It's over there mate. Hasn't moved all day'.

We were standing in a wood yard on the banks of the Thames staring across the water to the opposite bank where a swan was lying in the reeds.

'Can we climb up onto that wood pile to get a better look?' I asked.

'Course you can mate, but I tell you it must be mighty sick as it hasn't moved at all,' he reiterated.

Bob, my colleague joined me at the top and we concentrated at the white shape for a few minutes.

'What do you reckon Bob?'

'Looks like a swan to me and it could be dead'.

'I must admit it is difficult to see if it is moving'.

'I suppose we can't take the chance. We will have to go and see.'

'Any idea how we can get over there?' asked Bob.

'Nah mate. I reckon it will be difficult to reach that spot.'

The opposite bank was not industrialised, but just wild, as the river meandered tightly at this point in Canning Town, forming marshy promontories of long grass and reeds. There were no handy boats to try to hitch a lift across. Several men had joined us on the woodpile.

'Are you going to help the poor thing then?'

'We'll do our best if we can find a way over there.'

We returned to the van and perused the map book trying to discover the nearest road bridge and a way of approaching the spot. It was clear that there were no roads or tracks that would get us close. After nearly an hour of driving round we finally got as close as we could. We then had to cross a couple of footbridges and traipse through long grass and boggy ground until we were nearly opposite the wood yard. Some of the workers spotted us and started waving and shouting, but we were too far away to understand them. They began guiding us to the swan by pointing and gesturing. Bob and I split up so that we could approach along the bank from either side to give us a better chance of catching it if it made a dash for the water. We walked towards each other quietly and slowly, but couldn't locate the bird amongst the thick undergrowth and the workmen were frantically gesturing as though we were idiots. Finally, we were standing only six feet apart and at our feet lay a large white plastic sack. We looked from the bag to each other sheepishly.

'I told you it wasn't a swan,' I said.

'No I think I told you it wasn't.'

The men were jumping up and down wondering why we were not doing anything to aid the swan, so I picked up the sack and waved it over my head towards them. They appeared stunned for a few moments and then turned and shuffled out of sight.

*   *   *

London sustains a huge population of ducks and other waterfowl in its parks and waterways and they were regular customers. Spring and early summer were the worst periods for ducks as this was when the males grouped together to try to convince the females to mate with them. Unfortunately, this was mainly in the form of bullying them into submission. In any park you can see anything up to a dozen male ducks chasing a single female all over the place and not giving her a minute's peace. During courtship and mating, many females were half drowned or received raw wounds on the top of their heads from the males pecking at them or through flying into objects or cars in their effort to escape their unwanted advances. I once witnessed a poor female mallard duck being chased by six males, and as she half flew across a road in her bid to escape, she was hit head on by a car and killed in a cloud of feathers. The drakes stood and looked non-plussed for a while and then wandered off in search of another female to harass. We received dozens of telephone calls reporting bleeding, exhausted or fighting ducks and it was always difficult to explain that it was nature's way.

Once the courtship and mating is complete the ducklings arrive and there is more trouble. When female ducks protect their nests, they will often perform a curious decoy manoeuvre to distract any possible danger. They will pretend to have a broken wing or leg and hobble away in apparent distress in the opposite direction to the nest in order to distract you. People taken in by the ruse, would telephone us to come out and rescue it.

Some brainless females would choose rather strange places to build their nests and raise their young, often miles away from the nearest water. These individuals caused us problems each year, as they had a habit of nesting in the same place. I knew of a duck that insisted on nesting every year on the roof of St. Paul's Cathedral and another on the roof of a newspaper building in Fleet Street. The first year that the duck nested on the Fleet Street building was a disaster. When the time came to lead her offspring to water, she marched along the edge of the roof until she got to the end; she took off and the following youngsters tried to copy her, but plunged to their deaths. Two sensible souls amongst the brood, who were following up the rear, decided sensibly, not to follow their lemming siblings and stopped right on the edge. They wandered around chirping and teetering on the edge of oblivion, until a secretary in a building opposite spotted their predicament and contacted us. I managed to get onto the roof through a skylight and, whilst anxious office workers lining the windows opposite held their breath, I attempted to net them without driving them over the edge. It was all suspenseful stuff, but I managed to retrieve them. After that, we would come down each year and remove the ducklings before the mother took them on their suicidal march.

When the ducklings are old enough, the mother will lead them single file to the nearest pond or river by the shortest route. Female ducks have an amazing natural instinct to follow the shortest route to water, which can involve crossing busy roads, railway lines, shopping centres, roundabouts and all kinds of obstacles. If left alone she will get them to the destination relatively safely, but we would get flooded with calls when a mother decided to take her brood on a jaunt. I would plead with people to keep their distance and just assist the mother by escorting her and stopping traffic when necessary. This is really the best thing to do for the family, but well-meaning people would rush in, usually forcing the mother to fly off and leave a bunch of confused, panic stricken, chirping ducklings running around.

Ducks and ducklings were always getting into trouble

One morning, a duck was leading an unusually large brood along a busy part of the embankment by the Thames. She was disturbed and flew off leaving the ducklings behind. They were scooped up, placed in a cardboard box, and taken to Snow Hill Police Station. When I arrived, the Desk Sergeant presented me with the box. Snow Hill is a City of London Police Station and I always felt inferior when dealing with them, as all the constables had to be over six feet tall in order to join the force. Most seemed to exceed this requirement and with their unusually high helmets appeared very intimidating. Anyway, I took the box and I could not hear a sound from within until I opened the lid. Immediately twelve little yellow beaks and twenty-four black shiny eyes stared up at me and a crescendo of chirruping began. I have to say, that there is nothing cuter than these tiny brown and yellow fluff balls.

Caring for orphaned ducklings is quite an easy job and the success rate can be quite high, but they are messy little devils and can just die without warning. They should be kept under an infra-red lamp, which both warms them and keeps them dry. They can feed themselves from the point of hatching, but have a habit of climbing into their food and getting very wet and dirty. They want to swim, but they are not watertight at such a young age, so water must be dispensed in a container that does not allow them to jump in. Feeding is a selection of chick mash, finely chopped egg and grass fed very moist and they will hoover it up eating vast quantities. Then they have to be cleaned, as they will have managed to get most of the food over themselves. Most of this particular brood survived and were eventually released in a park.

* * *

It was a cold autumn day and I had just arrived at a wharf along the Thames at Limehouse. Some dock workers had spotted a small creature hanging on to a piece of driftwood for dear life. The animal was being slowly carried along by the incoming tide. They sprang into action and managed to rescue an oil soaked and half-drowned cat. I had been informed to go to the workers rest room, which turned out to be a large wooden hut. On entering, I found a group of men huddled round a gas fire. As they parted, I could see the small head of a cat peering up from beneath a towel. It looked utterly miserable and was shaking with a mixture of cold and shock.

'We've tried to warm 'im up and tried to get some milk down 'im, but he don't want to know', stated one of the men.

'Poor blighter is covered in muck and oil', added another man.

'Must 'ave swallared arf of the Thames,' agreed another.

'Lucky to be alive 'e is. Could 'ave been swept right away and drowned if old Joe 'ere hadn't spotted him', said the first one and all the men murmured in agreement.

They related the story of the rescue to me all trying to talk at the same time. They were really proud of their endeavours. Apparently, the cat had been hanging onto a broken wooden box with its front paws and only the head and shoulders were visible above the water line. Cats can swim, but are not as adept at it as dogs and also less inclined. The current, although not strong at the time, would have stopped him from making landfall so the game little thing had grimly hung onto the wood and left it to fate. Luckily, the workers had spotted the drama and managed to go to the rescue in a small outboard boat.

I gently lifted the towel and found underneath a sodden and almost steaming small black bundle of matted fur, which looked up at me with big sad eyes. I wrapped the cat up again and placed him into a basket.

'D'ya reckons he'll be orright?' asked one of the men.

'Thanks to you I'm sure he'll survive once he's had a clean and been dried out'.

'Let us know will ya, how he gets on like?' asked an almost embarrassed man.

'Of course I will,' I replied

All the men were obviously delighted with their efforts in saving the cat and as I left several of them shouted: 'good luck little fella'.

When I reached the surgery the 'little fella' had to undergo the indignity of a bath and when the oil and grime was removed, it transpired that it was not a he, but was in fact a beautiful black and white female. Although she was thought to be a year old she was delicate and small. Over the next few weeks she suffered from pneumonia and a bad bout of cat flu, but survived it all to emerge into a really cute cat. About a week after I telephoned the rescuers and informed them that their efforts had not been in vain and they were really pleased she had survived.

Having overcome all these ordeals it was only fair that she found a good home so I prevailed on my parents. On seeing her for the first time, they couldn't resist and immediately agreed to adopt her so she was soon on her way to a country village in Kent where she had the freedom of the house, my parents' shop and the garden. Her favourite place was always the shop where she soon had a large fan club amongst the customers. If not sunbathing in the window she was accepting compliments and strokes while perched on the counter. She had been given the nickname of "Oily" the day after her rescue and although we tried to rename her, this undignified title seemed to stick and she kept it for the rest of her life. Amazingly she lived for another twenty years: not bad for a bedraggled East End cat. The only consequence of her nightmare on the river was that she never liked faces near her and I often wondered whether she associated faces with all those workmen looming over her and staring down in that wooden shed by the Thames.

"Oily" relaxing in one of her favourite spots, a long way from the River Thames.

6:

The Night Shift

I battled through the rush hour traffic and finally reached Tavistock Square opposite Euston Station. This is a large London square near the British Museum, bordered with huge trees and in one of these, a commuter, on her way to the station, had spotted a pigeon hanging by its leg from a branch. Love them or loathe them, they are part of the London scene and when one was seen in distress most people could not pass the bird by without giving us a call. They might not want to physically help it themselves, but would salve their conscience by relying on us to help. I have to admit to a soft spot for them. Sure they can be messy, smelly, disease ridden and noisy, but they have an appeal, and that is why hundreds of people who sit in parks and squares to eat their lunch not only tolerate their presence, but actively encourage it, by sharing their food with them.

As I drove round the Square, I could see a group of about twenty commuters who had halted their usual rush to the Station, to stare up and point at the plight of the bird. I had obviously found my pigeon so I surreptitiously joined the rear of the crowd and looked up. The trees are very old and have a huge spread of branches and the bird was suspended by one leg from a branch some forty feet from the ground and 30 feet from the trunk.

Believe it or not, this was not unusual. Birds sometimes got bits of twine, string or cotton wound round their leg while they were wandering around on the ground. They then take off with this trailing from their foot and on landing the twine catches or wraps round a twig. When they try to take off again they come to an abrupt stop and find themselves hanging upside down by one leg. Some manage to get free by flapping their wings and struggling. Unfortunately, most of them remain trapped and over a period of time they gradually grow weaker, starve and die. I have seen trees in some London squares festooned with such dead birds, which from a distance look like hanging fruit bats.

Luckily it was autumn and the leaves had fallen making him easy to spot. I knew straight away that this one was going to be a problem as this was the highest hanging bird I had ever seen. The tree was too tall to climb and the branch too thin to get to the pigeon from the trunk. Every few seconds it would weakly flutter its wings and the assembled crowd of commuters, who would be normally rushing home and not stopping for anyone, were looking up with concerned expressions and murmuring "It's still alive" and "it won't last much longer". I was soon spotted and everyone turned to me with expectation. I immediately realised that there was no way I could rescue the bird alone and I required help. It was a Fire Brigade instruction to always telephone their control room, but as the fire station was just across the Euston Road I headed there. I felt rather embarrassed at these times, as I knew it was not really their job to rescue pigeons and they probably had far more urgent things to do, but the Station Officer I spoke to was very sympathetic.

'Sounds like a difficult one. We will be more than happy to assist, but I'll have to get onto our control for permission. Go back and show us where to stop and we'll be over right away,' he said enthusiastically.

It was a relief when they agreed to attend, which they invariably did. I often wondered what I would do in these situations if they flatly refused. I drove back to the tree and placated the bystanders with the announcement that help was on its way. A few minutes later the sound of a siren could be heard and a fire tender weaved its way through the heavy traffic and came to a halt next to my van. The road we were situated in was extremely busy at the best of times and with the rush hour in full swing the arrival of the fire engine started to cause a traffic jam. It also had the effect of attracting an even larger crowd of commuters. The Officer stood by my side and contemplated the pirouetting bird. After a discussion with his crew he turned to me.

'I'm afraid there is no way we can reach the bird. It's too high for our ladder and anyway the branch wouldn't take the weight.'

'I was afraid you would say that.' I confessed.

'All is not lost,' he said cheerfully, 'I think the answer is to call for one of our turntable ladders. Our's is in for repair, but we'll try and get hold of the one from our Soho station.'

With that he got into the tender and radioed his base. By this time the Police had turned up to see why there was such a crowd and why traffic congestion was so bad. It wasn't long before a siren could be heard in the far distance. A few minutes later, a large turntable appliance arrived, nudging the lines of traffic out of the way and blocking most of the road. More Police arrived, the traffic came to a standstill, the crowds swelled over the pavement and I began to think that everything was starting to get out of hand. I couldn't believe this was all happening for one pigeon. Well over thirty minutes had passed since my arrival and many of the original crowd had remained, totally enthralled by the proceedings and obviously determined to see it through to the end. The turntable ladder was driven into position with the Police directing the traffic out of the way.

'Want me to go up?' I asked quietly.

'No thanks. Only our lads are allowed to go up,' he replied. I breathed a sigh of relief, as I didn't fancy being the centre of attention.

The winch motor began to whine. I handed one of them a pair of scissors and a basket and he climbed into the cradle. Slowly the ladder made its way upward towards the stricken pigeon. In amongst the noisy traffic the crowd hushed. The fireman inched the cradle closer and closer to the bird. The sight of this made the pigeon panic somewhat and it proceeded to flap violently to get away. He gently grasped it and with a quick snip released it from its bondage. I half expected a loud cheer or applause from the assembled crowd, but none came. Everyone just turned and hurried off towards the station, chattering and laughing, obviously relieved that it had been rescued, but not wanting to delay their homeward journey any longer.

The pigeon reached the ground and I profusely thanked the firemen for their great efforts. They were eager to know if the bird was harmed in anyway, so I quickly checked it over. Often they could break a leg or the twine could cut the circulation and in this case the bird's foot was quite limp, but I informed them it should recover. They were really pleased and started to pack up all their gear. Apparently our little rescue had caused miles of traffic jams in all directions and, I have to admit, I loved it.

I decided to take the pigeon back to base, as he did not have a lot of feeling or grip in his foot. We removed the remaining twine successfully and the pigeon recovered the use of his foot and was released a couple of days later.

* * *

The night shift began at five in the afternoon when the receptionists, administration staff, telephone operators, vets, managers and nurses headed off home leaving the two emergency staff to man the fort until eight the next morning. A nurse also stayed until ten o'clock to attend to the animals in the hospital and any new arrivals during the evening. The first decision of the night was always which one of us was to be driver. As this was my favourite duty I was always eager for my colleague to volunteer for the less popular job of manning the telephones and reception.

When it was my night to drive, I was impatient for the telephone to ring and produce a call to go out on; not that I wanted an animal to be in pain or distress, but I knew that every shift there would be some unfortunate animal awaiting our help. I just wanted to be out there amongst all the hustle and bustle that was London; meeting wonderful and strange people; taking in the sights, helping animals in trouble and having adventures. If it was summer, then it was great to be driving round with the window open listening to the radio and watching the world go by. If it was winter then it was still fun, but I was less inclined for a long or messy rescue.

* * *

The rain was falling heavily, so hard in fact that the wipers were having difficulty in clearing it from the windscreen, making visibility very poor. The traffic jams were worse because everyone was slowing down and being careful, which was a change for London traffic. I arrived at what was probably the largest building site in London at the time. A huge area fenced off by corrugated iron and containing what was to become the new Barbican Centre with a Theatre, Museum, offices and apartments. I slithered to a halt in deep mud just inside one of the gates not daring to go any further in case I became stuck. I exited the van putting on my brand new, made to measure raincoat. In those days there was none of this off the peg rubbish. We would go down to the bespoke tailors of Hobson and Son just across the river in south London where we were measured for a complete uniform. It was all very posh and exciting and a few weeks later a large box would arrive containing a tunic, two pairs of trousers, a great coat, peaked cap and a raincoat, lovingly tailored to last for years. I had received the raincoat that day and I was really chuffed with it. It was the first time I had worn it and I reckoned it looked quite smart. Unfortunately the rain was so hard that it soon penetrated the coat as I struggled to put on my boots. I made slow progress over to a site office and was told to go to another hut further along. The whole area was littered with them and I was directed from one to another, slipping in the mud and dodging huge lorries that skidded by. Eventually I found the right one and escaped into the dry. A man looked up as I entered.

'Here to rescue the dog, eh? You've picked good weather for it,' he laughed.

I stood there, steaming and dripping, noticing splashes of mud all over my new raincoat.

'We reckon he must have wandered in looking for shelter and fallen into the trench. We've only just spotted him. Nobody fancied trying to get him out in case he was vicious. Poor thing needs rescuing as the trench is flooding.'

He donned a much more suitable raincoat and boots than mine and I followed him into the rain. The ground was a quagmire and the site manager led me some hundred yards and then pointed down into a trench.

'He's down there, mate.'

I carefully peered over the edge of a huge trench some ten feet deep and could just make out a dog huddled right at the end.

'Sorry but the only way down is that ladder at the end there,' he pointed out.

I approached with trepidation. Climbing down into a deep trench in the pouring rain was not my idea of fun and today it would have probably been against health and safety regulations. I slowly descended in my slippery boots and at the bottom found myself standing in a couple of inches of water, whilst more cascaded down on me from the sides. I cannot say I was enjoying myself at that stage and my hands and face were covered in mud and so was my lovely raincoat. I took a lead from my pocket and tried to make comforting noises over the sound of the rain. I half expected the dog to growl or lunge at me as I approached, but he just watched me with sorrowful eyes. As I got close to him he lifted his head and I could see he was quite a large black and tan cross breed German Shepherd. He was plastered in mud and soaked through. He was totally dejected and allowed me to loop the lead over his head.

I never went anywhere without a length of bandage in my pocket, so having retrieved it, I tied up his muzzle and again he made no effort to interfere. He really was one despondant dog. I had difficulty getting him to stand and walk through the water back to the ladder. Once at the foot it dawned on me that there was no way I could carry him up on my own. I stood at the bottom as miserable as the dog, with my boots gradually filling with water, while he slumped into the quagmire at my feet.

'I'm going to need some help,' I shouted up.

The site manager disappeared and a few minutes later four or five faces appeared above and stared down at me.

'If you can assure them he won't bite, they have volunteered to help,' he said laughing.

'Honestly he is fine. I have taped his mouth so he can't bite you,' I said to the peering faces 'If you don't mind I suggest you all take up position down the ladder and we can pass the dog to each other.'

The workmen did just that and my muddy companion made no effort to move a limb to help me lift him. He was a dead weight and I had to scoop him up into my arms getting water up the sleeves of my shirt and coat. I passed him up to the first man and he then did the same to the next, although this was more difficult than it sounds, as they didn't want to drop the dog and were not convinced he wouldn't struggle. Eventually our parcel of wet fur reached the top and we all clambered to the surface. We stood in a circle round him, all of us wet and miserable. I thanked everyone profusely and tried to head back to the van, but the dog wouldn't have any of it, so I had to carry him. By the time we got there I was exhausted and I placed him in the back where he flopped on the blanket and stared at me forlornly. I threw my brand new raincoat and boots in with him and I slumped into the front seat trying to dry my hair with a towel. It had not been the most enjoyable rescue. Back at the hospital he soon perked up after suffering the indignity of a bath and some welcome food. Unfortunately, no one came forward to claim him during his brief stay with us so he had to be transported to Battersea Dogs Home and his fate I never knew, but hopefully all our efforts were not in vain and he found a good home. Meanwhile, my lovely raincoat ended up at the dry cleaners.

* * *

Answering the telephone to the public, particularly where sick or injured animals were concerned, had to be one of the most stressful and frustrating occupations imaginable. I preferred to be out and about for this reason. The person responsible for telephones and reception had to keep a logbook. This involved noting the day and date, the names of staff on duty, the duty vet and the van mileage. After that, every telephone call or person arriving at the hospital was entered, with the reason they had called and what advice or action had been taken. This was also the same for the ambulance calls and late night surgeries. It was a wonderful record of events and it was fun to read what had happened to our colleagues on the opposite shift. It was almost a game to embellish and write humorous anecdotes of incidents that occurred, to provide everyone with a laugh.

It was always quieter in the winter than the summer, always quieter in bad weather than good weather and always quieter when there was a popular sporting fixture or programme on the television. It was generally busy early on, as we received calls from worried owners enquiring about the condition of their pets that had been admitted during the day for operations or treatment. There was a book often with a hundred separate reports from the five vets, on the condition of the patients. Normally it was good news, but often it could be bad news of an animal's death or requirement to be put to sleep: never a pleasant task to advise anyone. We also had owners coming in to collect their pets that were well enough to go home.

Once the early rush was over, telephone calls started coming in from people who had arrived home from work to discover their pets were sick. It was the main function of the person on telephones to filter out the emergencies from the non-emergencies and advise accordingly. By well-practised and astute questioning we gleaned what was actually wrong with the animal. Owners were notorious for exaggerating the condition of their pet and this was done either in an attempt to hoodwink you into believing it was an emergency so that you asked them in straight away or because they were just worried and panicking. Asking relevant questions to establish the actual symptoms the animal was really showing was almost an art form. Many people who worked and had busy lives much preferred to bring their animals in at night to save them taking time off work. Many did not take kindly to being told it could wait until the morning. Anything that we felt could not wait was referred to our emergency clinic, which was held at nine o'clock each evening.

The question of an owner's capability to afford a private vet was a constant problem area, as the RSPCA was a charity and technically was only supposed to treat the animals of owners who did not have the means to afford private fees. Deciding who was "poor" and who wasn't often led to heated discussions. I honestly felt then, and particularly now, that very few people fall into the poor category. There was nothing more annoying than to see an expensive car pull up and a well-dressed and manicured owner getting out followed by their pedigree dog. I knew in these circumstances that I was in for an argument. The problem was that they knew that if they made enough fuss and threats I would always put the animal's welfare above all other factors and give in.

As the evening progressed, it started to quieten down. Owners had collected most of the animals that were well enough to go home and it was too early for the emergency clinic clients. Out in the city motorists and pedestrians were spotting problems or actually causing them in their rush to get home and contacted us. The heavy volume of traffic resulted in numerous road accidents involving dogs and cats. In fact this was one of our most regular call outs in those days. Animal wardens had not yet been established and fewer tight controls meant there were far more stray and owned dogs left to roam the streets. The rush hour always proved to be a busy time. Commuters on foot often spotted injured animals in distress or trouble as they walked to the station or home.

The duty vet arrived just before nine o'clock and examined any patients we may have admitted, whilst we greeted patients destined for the emergency clinic. If it was quiet, we all sat in reception and enjoyed a chat and cup of coffee. During the normal working day, staff members were more circumspect with the veterinary surgeons as they were, of course, nominally in charge, but with the night staff there was always a strange "close" relationship between us. This was mainly because getting on the wrong side of us could result in busy nights for them as we were within our rights to constantly telephone them for guidance or actually call them out if we were so inclined. This of course we never did, as in general, we were in complete harmony with the vets and the system worked well. As a result, the vets tended to be very social with us.

When the Service moved from the old headquarters, it only used RSPCA employed vets, of which there were not many at the time. Five vets covered an evening each and took turns with the weekends. There was an apartment on the top floor of the hospital and at the time, a young vet named David resided up there who many years later became Veterinary Director and featured on the BBC Animal Hospital programme. However, when I first met him, he was a young graduate from the veterinary college, keen to get experience at the busy hospital. He was very useful to have on site, as in an emergency, we could telephone upstairs to see if he was in and ask for his help. He always came down to our rescue. There was a procession of young vets through the hospital, as it was the perfect training ground for them. They came from the College full of knowledge, but needed the practical experience. This they got at RSPCA Hospitals and Clinics, where they could see more types of animals and ailments and perform more operations and procedures in a month, than they could in a year at many private veterinary practices. Once the young vets had gained the experience they required, they left for private practice, where better career prospects and money beckoned. A keen young newly qualified vet would then join the ranks.

The number of patients arriving for the night surgery could vary between two and up to twelve depending on how successful we had been at weeding out the non-emergencies. Owners, who had used our service before, often turned up to the emergency clinic without telephoning first, as they knew a vet would be present. If we assessed them as a non-emergency and turned them away, then once again there could be conflict.

Just after ten in the evening the vet and nurse went home and we locked the front door. Many of the lights were doused to give some impression that we were not open for normal business. I greatly enjoyed this time. During the day, the hospital was a constant clamour of noise and bustle as five vets, twenty nurses and hundreds of members of the public made it arguably the busiest animal hospital in the country. After ten the hospital fell silent, we were alone with the animals, and it was one of the pleasurable duties to wander the wards checking that they were all happy and bedded down. On entering the wards, I was met by purrs, meows, yelps and barks of greeting. The occasional growl might be heard from a newly admitted dog that was sad, lonely and in pain. The sicker animals would be lying depressed on their blankets, gently moaning, with drips in their legs or lampshade like collars round their necks to stop them chewing out stitched wounds. Road accident cases had huge cumbersome bandages or plaster casts on their legs. Cats feeling much better and eagerly wanting to go home rubbed their faces and bodies along the wire cage fronts.

It would usually take a while to play with any puppies or kittens, scratch noses through the bars, give consoling words and catch up with the condition of accident cases we had rescued earlier. Once the lights were switched off, all was quiet.

This was also the time when people returning home from a night out often came across an animal that had been hit by a car, lying bleeding or comatose in a gutter or a front garden. They would telephone from a nearby telephone box or when they got home and the designated driver for the night headed off at speed to the address.

*   *   *

I slowly drove along the street looking from side to side for number 37. Apparently, a car had hit a ginger cat, some 30 minutes before, outside this address. Both sides of the street were lined with parked cars and the street was dimly lit. It was going to be a problem spotting it. Where possible, we always asked callers if they could stay with the animal until we arrived so that if it decided to drag itself away the person could see where it went to hide and lick its wounds. Failing that, we asked them to put a box or some kind of container over the animal or even take it indoors. Very few people though were able to do so and therefore we had to search for the cat when we arrived. Some people were very kind and took the animal into their house and I would find the cat or dog snuggled in a blanket in the kitchen awaiting my arrival. Many died soon after the impact and before I could get there, which was always very upsetting as dying alone and in pain was tragic. All I could do on arrival was to gently lift the body into a bag and hope an owner would telephone us reporting the cat lost. It is very sad for an owner to never know what has happened to a lost pet.

Cats involved in road traffic accidents were probably more of a problem than dogs. Injured ones were very adept at finding somewhere to hide following an accident. They tend to make a dash for it when crossing a road and shoot across at such a speed that invariably they suffer injuries to their hindquarters, normally a broken pelvis, or far worse, a fractured spine. With the front end still working it can travel large distances by dragging itself with its front legs: their stamina and fortitude is phenomenal. If the person who had reported the incident was still there on my arrival, it was great as they could point out where it was. Unfortunately, it was not the case on this occasion.

I pulled up, parked and retrieved my powerful torch, basket and grasper from the back of the van. There was no sign of blood in the road outside number 37. I started shining the torch along the gutter. There was no sign of a cat lying there. I then got on my hands and knees and started checking under each car. If it wasn't there, searching the front gardens was the next move. Sometimes we never did find the animal and had to presume it had made its way home or was lying hidden somewhere hopefully to be found later. At the sixth car, two eyes shone back at me in the beam of the torch. I had found a cat, but had to determine if it was the one I was looking for.

I edged closer under the cover of a few soft words until we were virtually eye to eye. At this point, if it wasn't badly injured, it would often make a run for it, particularly if it was feral and not used to human contact. On this occasion, it just remained crouched behind the back wheel of the car. I could see he was ginger in colour and I could see blood on his face so I knew I had found my road accident. The next problem was getting him into a basket. If a cat is in great pain or not that friendly, it can be a difficult operation for one person. I did not like using the grasper on them unless necessary and always tried to put a blanket right over the top of them or tried to grab hold of their scruff. I opened the lid of the basket in readiness and decided I couldn't be bothered to go back to the van and get the thick gloves. I would risk a bite or scratch as he seemed pretty relaxed having not hissed or growled so far. I did not think he intended any aggressive response so I slowly put my arm under the car and started to tentatively stroke his head with a finger. I was relieved when he didn't strike at me, and feeling confident, I slowly encircled the back of his neck with my hand. This was always the moment of truth and I grabbed his scruff and started to pull him out. He struggled slightly digging his paws into the tarmac in an attempt to remain under the car. I pulled slightly harder and he appeared. I then quickly put him in the basket, covered him with a small blanket and closed the lid. It had been an easy capture unlike many I had to attend to. When a cat is wild and striking out, the gentle approach was not always a good idea and it was less stressful all round just to get them into a basket by any means possible.

Cats can suffer horrific injuries in road accidents and are even more resilient than dogs. I have collected cats with an eyeball hanging out or a smashed lopsided jaw or a leg almost severed from the body and hanging by a sinew. Remarkably, they were often quite calm and showed no pain. Many I have rescued and returned to the hospital, I didn't expect to see alive again, but several days later, there they were lying in a cage in the ward, purring away with their injuries stitched or bandaged. Their power of recovery was astounding.

On busy nights, I could often get two or three emergency calls coming through at a time and had to speed from one to the other as quickly as possible, covering large distances in the process. It was always the way, that if more than one call was to come in, it would not be close to the other. This time I was lucky and had no further messages over the radio. With the cat safely ensconced, I headed back.

Once there I had to complete an admission form giving details such as the address found, the sex, colour, approximate age and then give the cat a thorough examination. Cats involved in road traffic accidents can suffer a variety of injuries depending on how hard they were hit and which part of their body received the impact. In this case, it was not too badly injured and turned out to be a neutered male ginger cat in good bodily condition. He was obviously well fed and looked after. His injuries proved to be minor: very shocked with a bloody nose and a little bruising. After a couple of days, he was back to full fitness and ready to go.

If an owner did not claim a cat, it was transferred to one of our animal centres and after seven days was put up for rehoming. They are not actually covered under the law and have no legal owner as such. Drivers do not have to report a road accident involving one, as you should with dogs. On some occasions, we felt that it was in the cat's best interests to find its own way home by returning it to where we had found it. This was always a difficult decision to make, because technically we were abandoning the animal and it could be embarrassing to be discovered by a member of the public appearing to be dumping a cat. Many people might argue it was not a sensible thing to do. I once came unstuck when I decided to release one late at night. I had just lifted it out and was trying to shoo him away when I suddenly spotted a woman approaching along the pavement. Seeing the RSPCA sign the woman was interested to know what I was up to. The cat had been rather confused at being released and was just sitting next to the basket with a puzzled look on his face. I had to quickly scoop him up again and put him back in. I muttered that I was just collecting an injured cat and then drove round the block before trying again.

As the ginger cat was obviously owned and well cared for, it was decided to return him to the scene of the accident. So three nights later, I took a chance and in the early hours, I drove him back to the street where I had found him. I looked up and down and there was no one obviously about. Having previously learned the lesson of never getting out of the van to release one, I had carried him on the passenger seat. I opened the door and let him jump out. He sniffed the air for a few seconds, looked round to get his bearings and then scurried into a garden. Hopefully owner and cat were reunited in the morning.

Late at night when I drove round the deserted streets and wandered the dark, dingy and dirty blocks of flats on the awful housing estates, the derelict wharf areas and the old bomb sites, I never felt frightened or uncomfortable. It never struck me that it might be a dangerous environment in which to be alone. When I drive round London now and see the apartment doors covered in metal cages and padlocks, the gangs of kids hanging around, I somehow don't feel I would be so nonchalant.

Once we had completed our late night jobs, we retreated to our cosy little night room on the first floor, almost above the front door. We made a cup of tea, turned on the television, reduced the lighting to one table lamp and settled into our chairs to await events.

This was the time when it was difficult for people to contact their own private vets. All of them had to provide a twenty-four hour service and give emergency first aid to an animal regardless of the ability of the owner to pay. This was written in their charter and code of practise, but at that time, many surgeries were one man bands, and they could not be expected to be on twenty-four hour call every day, so they had to pair up with another local surgery to share the out of hour's service. This was not always possible, and even when there was such an arrangement, the covering vet might be out on a call and not available to answer the telephone. In these circumstances, it became a headache for us. Some local surgeries not only wouldn't see anyone who could not afford their fees in an emergency, but often declined seeing their own clients out of hours as well. Unfortunately, there was the odd one who had a habit of mistakenly turning off his telephone or not answering it during the night. If they did answer, they sometimes quoted a high fee to avoid being called out. Some would even recommend calling us. I had one incident where a vet turned away a road accident animal from his doorstep that required expensive treatment when they realised the owners might not be able to pay the fees.

Because we did answer our telephone, we occasionally had arguments with worried pet owners as we insisted they persevered in trying to contact their own vet. It reached the point sometimes when I had to try to contact the vet on their behalf and insist that he helped his client. Some owners, who did not want to pay the expensive out of hour's fees, would insist their vet was not available even though he was. In these cases, I would call him on our second line and then inform the irritated owner that their vet was awaiting a call from them. It was all a bit of a game, but unless we did it, there was no way we could have coped with the volume of animals requiring help. Taking in animals of owners that could afford would have taken up the time, drugs, and space we required for the stray animals we were mainly there for. In those days, the quality and conscientiousness of some private vets and their out of hour's service had a lot to be desired. The situation is far better today, as vets pay private companies to cover their out of hour's service or are large enough to cope themselves and the introduction of pet insurance makes it less of an issue as the bill is paid by them.

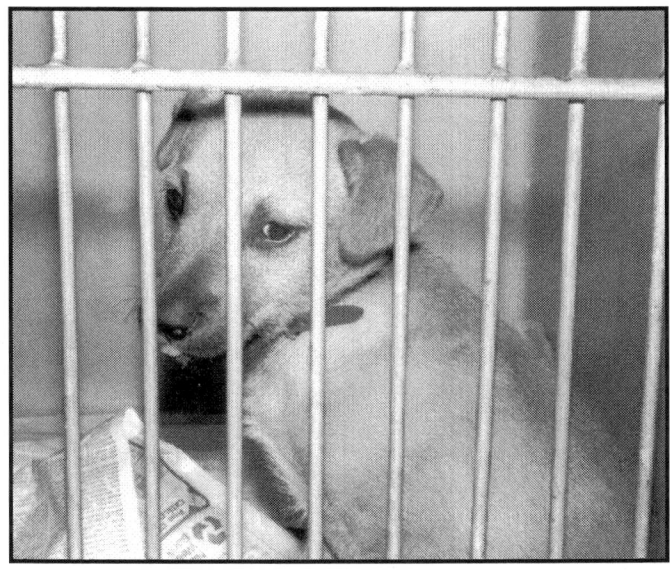

One of the most pleasurable duties at night was to wander the wards bedding down the animals.

When owners arrived at the door during the night in a worried or panicked state it was surprising how few of them queried the fact that there was no vet present and trusted me to attend to their beloved pet. Dealing with the situation calmly and with assurance, I believe offset any worries they might have had. They wanted their pet to be helped and if this was being done, they were happy. On occasions, they did stand their ground and refuse to leave until they had seen and spoken to a vet. If the animal was in need of hospitalisation, the trick was to part them from their pet as quickly as possible. I would urgently usher them into the consulting room and take their details, then question them on the history and symptoms the animal was suffering from.

Examining the animal was the next step and made the owners feel I was at last doing something to help. Taking the temperature was a good start. Most dogs and cats have a normal temperature of around 101.5 degrees. Any higher or lower than this indicates a fever or infection or determines whether the animal might be in shock. If the pupils are of different size it can give an indication of brain damage, if small, it might be concussion and if they are jerking around in the eye, it could be sign of poisoning or trauma. The membrane or third eyelid protruding across indicates that an animal is generally feeling under the weather and when the gums are pale, the animal could be suffering from shock, low blood pressure or loss of blood.

When a cat has fallen from a height it often suffers a split palate where the roof of the mouth literally splits from back to front and if the jaw is fractured it wobbles from side to side and there might be missing or chipped teeth. An accident case that is sitting hunched, with its tongue hanging from an open mouth is an indication it may have suffered a ruptured diaphragm from the impact. This is where the small intestine or stomach protrudes into the chest cavity. It is distressing for them in this state, as the poor thing will be trying to get air by breathing from its stomach.

Paralysis of the hind legs and tail can mean a fractured spine, nerve damage or a fractured pelvis. After an accident or a bad bite, cats can suffer radial paralysis where the nerve running down the front leg is damaged and it loses feeling. Fractured or broken bones were obvious to spot and torn or shredded claws were an indication of an animal being dragged along under a car.

This sounds as though it took forever to check all these things, but in fact, it could be done in a few minutes, as many symptoms were obvious. At the end of all this I had a pretty good idea of what was wrong with the animal and I either admitted it to be looked at by the vet in the morning or the owner was offered advice and sent away. If I felt it needed the urgent intervention of drugs or treatment I would leave the owner in the consulting room and go to the office and telephone the vet for advice. I would relay the detailed symptoms and what I thought might be wrong. The vet then told me what treatment to give and what to say to the owner. I would breeze back into the consulting room, pick up, fill syringes, and inject the animal while giving assurances to the owners.

I then took the animal to an appropriate ward, waking up all the other inmates in the process when I entered and switched on the lights. That done I scooted back to the owners and ushered them to the door telling them to telephone later that morning for an update.

Then it was a question of completing all the paperwork, placing it on the cage front and adding the patient to the observation or operating list for the vet to see in the morning. Another emergency dealt with.

I once came unstuck, when advising an owner of what treatment we intended carrying out on their pet, which was suffering from shock following a road accident. Being late at night, during a long weekend shift, when my brain was not in top gear, I had apparently said to the owner that we were going to give the animal shock treatment. The owner must have gone home and mulled this over, because next day she telephoned in a complaint to the deputy chief vet at the hospital. When I next came in on duty, I was summoned to the veterinary director's office where I was torn off a strip for telling the owner I was going to electrocute her dog. At first I thought he was joking, but apparently not, and forever after I always made sure that I said we would be giving the animal 'treatment for shock!'

The saddest part of the job was when a pet arrived dead. Breaking such news to the owners was always an emotional strain and some needed a lot of convincing that their beloved pet was definitely dead. An animal that has life in it will always have a reflex in the eye. I would check by lightly touching the corner of the eye with the tip of my finger. The animal always blinked or twitched the eye if it was alive. Eyes that are glazed over or do not react to light, lack of a heartbeat and gums that are white are a sure sign that the animal has passed away. It is possible to give artificial respiration to animals by pressing down lightly on the heart with the palm of your hand or giving mouth to nose resuscitation by cupping your hands round the animal's muzzle and blowing.

By about one or two in the morning, we were always looking forward to getting our heads down for four or five hours uninterrupted sleep before the day staff started to arrive. This rarely happened as more often than not there were at least two or three telephone calls during the early hours and there were often occasions when I had to go and attend an early morning call out.

*   *   *

It was about five o'clock in the morning and I was driving through the completely deserted streets to Smithfield Meat Market. I had been called there to collect what had been described as an unusual bird they had found. The market opens at a very inconvenient time of 3 a.m. and so if I ever had to go there it was always going to be early. Anyone can buy from the market, but you have to arrive by 7 a.m. to grab a bargain. There has been a market on the site for over a thousand years, but the present one was opened in 1867. It is a huge old building with a gigantic 225-foot glass domed roof. There were several cafes, which opened early to accommodate the market workers, and a hearty breakfast could be obtained. I had often stopped in the past when passing to obtain a bacon sandwich or two.

As I neared, the traffic increased and I was soon fighting my way through the lorries delivering their loads of meat and poultry from all over the country. It was always quite hazardous with lorries suddenly stopping and then reversing up to the unloading ramps. You also had to avoid wooden carts being pulled at break neck speed by the porters. Huge sides of meat seemed to be constantly gliding around the market, carried by men called 'humpers', 'pitchers' and 'porters' depending on which part of the carrying process they were involved in. Men dressed in blood stained white coats chopped and carved with large knives and cleavers, their hands protected by chain mail gloves. It was all very macabre.

I had difficulty finding somewhere to park and even when I did find a small space; drivers tooted their horns to make me move. I finally tucked the van between two trucks and hoped it would not be damaged by the time I got back. Being such a close-knit community, everyone was aware that the RSPCA was on its way and when I pulled up and got out of my marked van the good-humoured banter and innuendo began.

''ere Ernie, they've come to collect you mate,' someone shouted to his workmate. This was greeted by a lot of laughter.

'Nah, he's come to put old Frank down,' shouted another 'you're a right old animal aren't you Frank?'

'That's what his missus reckons, anyway. Eh, Frank?' Cue even louder laughter.

'You can collect my missus anytime and put her down, mate,' someone else shouted to me.

Same old jokes but all good fun. I just wished they were not all so lively and awake at that time of the morning.

'Go and see Stan at Number 509 mate. He knows where the bird is,' I was helpfully told.

Inside the building, there were rows of partitioned stalls with green signs above giving the name of the Company and the number. I wandered up the alley between them pushing past the throng of buyers. I watched as stallholders stood on boxes and offered meat up for sale and buyers shouted offers to buy. I finally found Stan who like many others was standing there in his blood stained white coat.

'Come for the bird have you lad? Follow me,' he shouted over the din.

He led me out to the back where the trucks and vans were unloading.

'Yeh, we found him sitting among the empty boxes when we were unloading earlier. I think it's an owl.'

'An owl!' I exclaimed 'It would be very unusual to find one here.'

'Well several of the lads have seen it and we all reckon the same'. Stan showed me a pile of old boxes stacked against the wall of the building. 'He's hiding behind one of them at the top. We have tried not to disturb him, but he doesn't seem fussed about all the noise.'

The pile was some seven or eight feet high and they had just been thrown on top of each other. I did not want to disturb them too much in case they all tumbled down. I slowly and quietly walked over to them and on tiptoe peered amongst them. I suddenly saw two round yellow eyes staring back at me. Sitting quite happily in an upturned box was a small owl no bigger than my hand. I turned to Stan.

'You are right. It is an owl. I wonder how on earth it got here.'

Stan was obviously pleased that his bird identification skills had been correct and he slightly puffed out with pride at my congratulation. He also wanted to prove that he was a bit of a detective as well.

'The lads and I reckon that somehow he got trapped or fell into the back of a lorry and got brought here from who knows where.'

'I think you may be right. I'll just go back to the van and get my gloves and a basket.'

When I returned, I slowly reached up and the owl just followed my outstretched hand with his bright round eyes and bobbed his head up and down. He didn't seem perturbed and in fact just allowed me to pick him up. I had gathered a small audience by this time and the group of men, who looked like a band of blood-splattered pirates, gathered round me.

'It is actually a species called a Little Owl,' I announced to them.

I then carefully examined the beautiful creature. It had a rather squat appearance with a flat head, speckled chest and a thin black beard running along his chin. He stared up at me and the assembled men were fascinated. I stretched his wings one by one and discovered that one was fractured and hung down slightly.

'I'm afraid he has a broken wing. He was probably hit by the lorry and ended up in the back,' I suggested.

'You are not going to kill it are you mate?' pleaded one of the men.

'Of course not, I'm sure we can mend it I replied.'

They all seemed satisfied with this and went back to their bloody work. I put the owl in the basket and carried him back through the market towards my van. I had to constantly stop to show the bird to other concerned market men who wanted to see it and be assured that I was not going to kill it. In fact, we were able to mend the wing and I took the owl home to recuperate. He was eventually released in the countryside of Kent.

*   *   *

If we were not already awake dealing with a telephone call, the early staff woke us every morning by ringing the night bell and I would trudge bleary-eyed downstairs to let them in. It was then a case of checking the animals we had admitted during the night and explaining the previous night's events to the day staff. Once that was done, I headed for the animal kitchen to get a bottle of milk for the all-important morning cup of tea. In the animal kitchen, a ward nurse spent an hour or more conjuring up all kinds of tempting food for the animals, the aroma of which made you either hungry or nauseous depending on how you felt that morning. There were bowls of pilchards and sardines in tomato sauce; large vats of fish, minced meat and rice boiling on the stove along with saucepans of chicken stock, gravy and porridge. Tins of dog and cat food and tins of special liquid diets had to be opened. Powdered milk had to be mixed along with special supplements and slices of bread. There might be a bowl of maggots for the fledglings if you were lucky! With over a hundred inpatients, ranging from dogs and cats to birds and wild animals the preparation of a menu to suit all was quite a task to perform each morning. In no time at all the wards were a whirl of noisy activity as the animals were fed, cleaned out and treated. The hospital was up and running again for another day and our part was over, until we had to return that afternoon to do it all again.

7:

Dogs in Trouble

Trying to negotiate traffic down the Whitechapel Road in East London was always a nightmare. It was a long way from Finsbury Park and I had already taken an age trying to reach the scene of a road accident. Finding my way around London was not a problem, as I knew all the back doubles, one way systems and short cuts. It was a dark, cold and damp evening, which always made driving more difficult. Bow Road Police had reported a dog that had been hit by a car and was apparently lying in the road near the market stalls that line that part of the road during the day. I was frustrated not to be able to plough through the traffic, although I did drive rather aggressively in these circumstances, hoping other road users would appreciate that I was in a hurry for a purpose.

When I arrived at the scene of a road accident, there was often a crowd of concerned onlookers. Although they were aware that I did not have blue lights or sirens in order to speed me to the emergency, it did not stop them chiding me for taking so long to arrive and leaving the animal to suffer. Sometimes a traffic jam of frustrated drivers had to be negotiated in order to reach the animal. On this occasion, there was no crowd or traffic jam and as I pulled up there was no dog. Usually it was in the middle of the road or still under the wheels of the vehicle. The Police had disappeared along with the driver of the car. Again, this was not unusual if it had taken a while to attend. Although the Police were responsible under U.K. law to deal with injured and stray dogs, they rarely if ever could be bothered in London at that time, as they knew we would deal with the problem and, more importantly, pick up the cost. Getting out of the van I was approached by a market stallholder, who was packing up for the night.

'It's limped down that alley mate. Everyone went when it scarpared off the road.'

'Is it badly injured?' I asked.

'Dunno mate, but rather you than me as it's a really nasty piece of work.'

I often faced this scenario. It was no fun being alone down an alley in the dark with an unpredictable dog in pain. I grabbed a torch, the ever-dependable grasper and I slowly walked down the alley shining the torch at all the crates, and boxes discarded by the market people and crammed along the sides. The word had obviously gone round and there was a collection of locals watching me, probably hoping for some excitement. Twenty yards in, I heard a quiet growl and I saw the dog lying beside some of the discarded boxes. If not badly injured, it is not unusual for them to limp off to lick their wounds in a quiet place.

I crouched down about eight feet from the dog and quietly spoke to him. It was always a good move to crouch as I appeared less threatening and a few soft words often, but not always, had a calming effect. Gradually I edged my way nearer to him, stopping every time he growled. After a good five minutes, I was kneeling beside him, chatting away like some idiot and, although growling softly, he seemed to be tolerating my presence. It was time to try to get hold of him. This was always the decisive moment, as I never knew how a dog would react. Would he run, try to bite or accept my help? In the light of the torch, I could see he was a typical East-End mongrel. Of no particular breed, medium sized, black and tan in colour and wearing no collar. He was shaking with a combination of fear and shock. I slowly removed a bandage from my pocket, not to dress his wounds, but to make a muzzle.

This was one of the first tricks I learned when joining the RSPCA and something at which I became very adept with practise. I tore a strip about three feet or so long and then slowly tied a slipknot half way along leaving a loop eight inches in diameter. I then leaned over the dog and dangled the loop near his nose. The idea is to get this over the nose, pull it tight, and then to tie the bandage round a couple more times before tying the bandage behind his neck. Definitely easier said than done, as the first instinct of the dog is to lower or turn his head every time you try to get the noose over its nose. It can take a lot of patience and time, but it is very important to get a muzzle on as animals in great pain and trauma often strike out at those trying to help them. Eventually I managed to get the bandage round his nose and I gently tied it off. I then gingerly put my hands under his body while he watched me wide-eyed, the whites of his eyes, standing out in the darkness. He hardly made a whimper and I slowly lifted him and carried him back to the van amongst polite applause from the assembled onlookers. On the way back I chatted to the dog assuring him he was going to be OK. It was something I always did when I had injured animals on board. Silly maybe, but I liked to think it made them feel better and calmed them. I liked to transport seriously injured small dogs and cats on the passenger seat as I could keep an eye on them and physically comfort them as well. He was later found to have a fractured hind leg and remained with us for over a week before being transferred to Battersea Dogs Home.

*   *   *

Dealing with road accident dogs was always a case of acting with care and calm. Knowing its demeanour was always a problem and often solved by the time I arrived, as either someone was happily holding onto it or had already been bitten. Well-meaning spectators instinctively rush in to help an animal they see hit by a car, little realising that it does not always appreciate a complete stranger suddenly looming over it when it is frightened and in pain. I once attended a dog which had dragged itself to the gutter. A young woman who witnessed the accident rushed over to give it help and it lashed out. When I arrived there was an ambulance attending to the woman who nearly lost a finger because of her concern. It is best to approach these animals with great care. An apparently friendly injured animal can soon become snappy when you try to move it and perhaps cause pain. If it is impossible to secure the dog's nose then a thick blanket or coat over the head can prove a good substitute. It is no joke having to bend over a strange dog in pain with your face so close to its mouth.

Little first aid can be done when attending to one lying in the street except for applying a tourniquet or bandage on a badly bleeding wound. It is important to try to discover where the blood is coming from. When a vein is cut, the blood is crimson in colour and flows or seeps out, but if an artery is cut, the blood is scarlet and literally spurts out. In the dark, it is often difficult to properly examine an injury. I have seen animals sustain horrific injuries, which would kill a human being, but they have survived. It is important to get the animal to a vet as soon as possible.

Initially, it is shock that is the main enemy and checking the degree of shock is relatively simple and is a case of pressing the gum above the teeth. A normal gum will be quite pink and when pressed with a finger will go white as you force the blood away. When the pressure is removed, the blood should rush back immediately. An animal in severe shock will have low blood pressure and therefore have pale or even white gums and there will be little or no change in colour by putting pressure on the gum. Covering a dog with a blanket to keep it warm and turning up the heating in the van would always help them perk up and feel more comfortable.

Dogs suffer head injuries as either they are hit head on by a car or their hindquarters are injured as a car swerving to avoid them clips their rear end. If hit on the head, the dog often bites through its tongue making it bleed profusely. This makes the injury look far worse than it really is. Other injuries included a nosebleed, concussion or a bloody eye. If hit full on they can be horrifically dragged under the car ripping away large flaps of skin and causing bruising and wounds that are full of road grit and dirt. Cars clipping their hindquarters cause fractures to the pelvis or legs and in the worst cases fracture the spine resulting in paralysis. All these injuries need x-rays and operations under anaesthetic, which can only be done once the animal is over the shock and more settled. Shock can be a killer in itself so when all around were in a state of panic, I knew the best thing to do was to quietly return the animal to the vet for examination and to let the animal rest.

*   *   *

We were suddenly awoken with a start from our afternoon stupor as the front doors of the hospital crashed open. It was a very hot Sunday afternoon, the telephones had stopped ringing and we had been drifting off.

'You have got to help us. Our dog is dying,' screamed a man.

The man and his wife were valiantly trying to carry a large comatose dog in their arms.

'What's the problem?'

'He collapsed in the heat. We only left him a short while in the car, but he was collapsed when we got back.'

We grabbed a trolley, basically a metal stretcher on wheels similar to those in a human hospital and we laid the dog on it.

'Now stay here a moment,' we told the distraught owners, 'we need to attend to the dog quickly. You can come through in a minute.'

'But we want to stay with him,' they pleaded.

'I'm sorry, but it is best you stay here,' we insisted.

In emergencies, it is always wise to separate the owner from the animal, as it can get rather fraught at times. With that, we quickly pushed the trolley through the double doors into the inner sanctum. The reception and telephones were abandoned, as it was more important in these cases to concentrate on the seriously ill patient. We hurtled down the corridor past the operating theatres, skidded sharp right down the back corridor past the dog wards. Being high summer the dog ward windows and doors were all open and the inpatients all started barking at the commotion. We wheeled left down another short corridor into the animal kitchen. A strange place to take a seriously ill dog you might think, but in the kitchen, we had a huge walk in fridge with a concrete floor.

I then examined the animal for the first time to confirm what I already knew to be the problem. It was a large shaggy crossbreed and he was almost unconscious with a glazed look in his eyes. He was not responding to us and was panting noisily, convulsing and salivating. His legs were stiff and by touching his body and nose, he was boiling up. I knew he was suffering from heat stroke and I needed to do something quickly or he would die. My colleague quickly cleared out the milk crates and boxes from the fridge and we lifted him down to the floor. The nurse appeared with a thermometer and inserted it into his rectum while my colleague filled a bucket with cold water and soaked the towels in it. Removing the thermometer, we discovered that the dog's temperature was 106 degrees Fahrenheit. A normal temperature would be around 101.5. A bowl of cold water was poured over him, followed by the wet towels and some ice obtained from the staff kitchen. We continued to make him as cold as possible even running a hose pipe in through the back door to keep a constant stream of cool water trickling over him. The fridge was a complete mess by now and water was running across the kitchen floor, but it was important to get his temperature down. Our duty vet was telephoned and the nurse gave the dog some medication. I kept checking his temperature and was pleased to see that it was beginning to come down. He started to respond to all our efforts and so I went and got the owners explaining why we had their pet soaking wet in a fridge. In these circumstances, it was tempting to have a go at them for their stupidity and the suffering they had put their pet through, but the sight of him was enough to make them feel guilty. On this occasion, the dog survived and was later put in a cage with a fan to keep him cool.

There are a small percentage of dog owners who never appear to learn about looking after them in hot weather. If the driver or passengers are feeling hot, driving in their car it should be obvious to anyone that leaving a living thing inside a stationary vehicle on a hot day is not a good idea. After a dog has nearly baked to death, owners will often excuse themselves with: "Well, we left a couple of windows slightly open" or "we parked the car in the shade." Opening windows or the skylight has no real effect at all, as heat builds up quickly with the sun beating down on a car, particularly if it is humid.

Dogs cannot sweat like humans to cool down and they have to pant to try to expel some of the heat. However, this is not a very efficient method of cooling them down if the dog cannot escape the heat. It is the same if left in a conservatory, shed or kennel or any circumstance where heat can build up in an enclosed airless space. Longhaired dogs obviously suffer far worse, but heat stroke can affect rabbits and guinea pigs too.

As the heat builds up the dog starts to pant and it hangs its tongue out in an attempt to cool down and gradually the panting gets worse until it starts to salivate. Then the dog will start to stagger and fall over and the eyes become glazed. If the heat increases further or the dog is left for a long time the symptoms get so pronounced that it collapses and loses consciousness. By this time, the dog's temperature will rise from 101 degrees up to as much as 110 degrees. It is an agonising experience if it survives, and a terrible way to die. If I was an owner who caused so much suffering, I could never forgive myself, but many got antagonistic when confronted by their stupidity.

Usually it was RSPCA Inspectors who attended dogs shut in cars due to the legal aspects, but in an emergency, I occasionally attended such incidents. I remember two in particular, as I was so pleased with the police response. I was called to a car parked on the Inner Circle Road near London Zoo. On arrival, I could plainly see that the dog was in some distress as he was panting violently. I got on the radio and asked my colleague to telephone for Police assistance. We were not allowed to break into cars so we had to call them. Within ten minutes, a panda car turned up with two officers and luckily, one of them was a dog lover. He was incensed that someone had left the dog and immediately agreed to gain access. By using a piece of wire poked through the slightly open window, he managed to hook the catch and open the door. We had just got the dog out and given him some water that we had scrounged, when the owners turned up with the usual excuses. They were annoyed that we had entered their car, which irritated the Policeman even more. He tore into them and gave them a wonderful telling off and warning.

On another occasion, I was called to a car parked near Hampstead Heath in the full sun with no window open. There was a greyhound type dog inside and I could see he was on the point of collapse. This time it was a Police dog handler who turned up and he was as concerned as I at the condition of the dog. He tried for ages to open the door and even called for backup. They slid a length of wire down between the rubber of the window and the frame to try to release the lock on the door without success. The dog meanwhile was getting worse and eventually one of the officers turned to me and asked 'would you say that he is suffering and in imminent danger of dying?'

Well I had no authority really to make such a decision, but I replied 'Yes, I would say so.'

'That's good enough for me,' stated the Police officer and he proceeded to smash one of the windows. It was great, as I love direct action and I felt it would teach the owner a lesson. Again, whilst I was examining and giving him water, the owners turned up. They went berserk about the state of the car and insisted they had only been gone a short time. The Police Officer wouldn't have any of it, pointing out that we had been there for nearly half an hour trying to get the dog out. A terrific argument ensued and I was worried I might be liable for the damage, but the dog recovered and I took the opportunity to disappear. I never heard any more about the incident and presumed the Police sorted it out. Forty years on and depressingly, some owners still do not show common sense and they are still left in cars on hot days.

* * *

Each shift we were confronted with a variety of injuries to dogs that required us to give first aid, treatment or advice. Burns and scalds frequently occurred when pets got under the feet of their owners in the kitchen. They would trip over them whilst carrying a pan of hot water or oil and this would spill over the animal causing scalding. It was also common in winter for animals to get too close to an electric or open fire and be scalded. In both cases, it was best to immediately pour water over the affected area to flush away whatever was spilt. Fat was particularly bad as when it cools it can solidify and seal the heat in making the burn worse. The fat must be removed immediately. Ice cubes in a bag or good old frozen peas are useful in reducing the heat in the wound, which lessens the damage done to the skin cells. On rare occasions, chemicals, such as tar, paraffin, petrol or household cleaners, could burn animals. Treatment for these burns was more specific to the actual cause. Acidic burns required cleaning with bicarbonate of soda or washing soda. Alkaline burns, like caustic soda, required cleaning with vinegar and water and oil or petrol with something like Swarfega.

Dogs can suffer a variety of accidents whilst playing with their owners. Chasing after a stick too quickly can lead to it jarring into their mouths, cutting the inside and making it sore and painful. Parts of the stick might break off and get wedged between the teeth or in the roof of the mouth. It is important when playing ball with a dog to make sure it is not too small and likely to get lodged in the back of the throat. If it does, it can restrict the airflow and become life threatening. Trying to poke the ball or obstruction can make matters worse as it can be pushed further down. It is better not to throw a ball up too high and use a tennis size one.

Some accidents and injuries were very bizarre. Back then, leads mainly had a spring clip at the end unlike the trigger most leads have today. In their excitement to go out for a walk, a dog often trod on the clip and the weight pressed it open forcing it to catch on the most painful part of its paw: the tender web of skin between the toes. The dog often panicked in these circumstances and hurtled round the house trying to rid itself of the lead. Owners turned up having been unable to remove the clip, as every time they tried the dog would go mad with the pain. Nine times out of ten, the animal had to be admitted for an anaesthetic to remove it.

On occasions, dogs were bitten by snakes, which isn't a problem if bitten by the non-venomous Grass Snake. The Adder on the other hand is venomous and a bite from one of these can cause a painful swelling and considerable distress. If a dog proves particularly allergic or is a small breed, it can cause difficulty in breathing and even collapse. The only first aid is to wash the wound with soap and water and keep the animal still until you can reach a vet. Few people know that dogs can be poisoned by grabbing hold of Common Toads. The toad secretes protective venom over its body if attacked which causes the dog to salivate and become distressed. Given the chance, cats love to chase frogs and toads as well.

An animal suffering a fit is probably the most distressing situation to witness and most occur in dogs. The dog loses consciousness and thrashes about on the floor often quite violently. They will make paddling, walking or running motions with their legs or fall over in fixed frozen spasm. They might champ their jaws, froth and salivate. An elderly dog that suddenly collapses, convulses and becomes unconscious with open staring eyes is probably having a heart attack. Its tongue and lips will go blue. Many dogs can be epileptic and certain breeds, such as German Shepherds, are prone to this. Poisoning can sometimes cause fits.

In nearly all cases, fits only last for a few minutes, but during that short time, they are a frightening experience for both owner and animal. The first thing to do is to put it in the dark and quiet, wrapped up in a blanket or wedged with cushions so that it cannot do any harm to itself while thrashing about. This was always the advice I gave over the telephone when terrified owners called me. Unfortunately, many would not heed the advice as they thought their pet was dying in agony and would rush it to the hospital. This made matters worse and often extended the fit. When they arrived with the dog thrashing in their arms, I did exactly what I had recommended over the telephone, much to the owner's chagrin, as they expected some intensive treatment to be given.

*   *   *

As I turned into the street, all I could see were fire engines and ambulances. There was smoke billowing from a ground floor flat as I got out of the van and headed towards the action. As I passed the ambulance, I could see a stocky man sitting on the back step. His face and arms were blackened as was his vest and shorts. A firefighter noticed me staring at the man and approached.

'He's the culprit. Lucky not to be badly injured,' he said.

'What happened?' I asked.

'There has been an explosion. The idiot was cleaning the petrol tank of his motorbike on the kitchen table and the fumes were ignited by the gas stove,' he smiled. 'Shouldn't laugh, but it's hard not to.'

'I understand he had a dog?' I enquired.

'Yep, A German Shepherd. It was in the kitchen with him and caught the blast as well.'

'Is it OK?'

'Somewhat singed I would say. I'll show you where it is.'

It appeared that the man had decided it was a perfect sunny afternoon to do some maintenance work on his motorbike. He had removed the petrol tank, taken it into his kitchen, and placed it on the table. His faithful dog had lain next to him. The fatal mistake had been to turn the gas cooker on to make a cup of tea. The fume-filled room had ignited and exploded. I followed towards the smoking flat and I could see another fireman hanging onto a very wet and dejected looking dog, near one of the fire tenders.

'Hope we did the right thing, but he was actually on fire when we found him so we drenched him with water.'

'No, that's fine. It's the best thing to do.'

Even though it was a hot summer afternoon, the dog was shivering from shock. The poor thing was in quite a state with a lot of his fur singed and blackened. There were raw patches of bright red flesh where the burning had penetrated.

'He is in quite a mess. I had better get him back to the vet as quickly as possible.' I went to the van, got a blanket, and asked if they could soak it with water for me, which they did. The dog was remarkably well behaved considering the pain and discomfort he must have been in. I think the shock had subdued him. His gums were almost white, a sure sign that he was in severe shock. I got him into the back with the help of a fireman and then gingerly laid the wet blanket over him. I winced when I did this, as I was not sure how he would react and I knew it must be painful. For the first time he reacted by whimpering and thrashing around, but I finally got him settled. The cooling effect of the blanket lessened the pain and took the heat out of the burns, therefore reducing the damage done. I could see the ambulance pulling away with the owner on board.

'They are taking him to hospital as he has burns like the dog,' said a fireman.

'Can you get the Police to tell him where his dog is,' I asked.

'Sure thing.'

I then put my foot down and drove, as quickly as possible back to the hospital. Severe scalding and burns and the associated severe shock can be fatal. At the hospital, he was heavily sedated to help his pain and we gave him treatment for shock, put him on a drip and carefully cleaned the charred skin and hair from his wounds with a salt solution. Then any raw patches were gently covered with a dressing. The dog did recover slowly and left the hospital a week later.

*   *   *

With so many dogs running round excitedly in the parks, it was always a matter of time before fights broke out and they regularly arrived on our doorstep shocked and bleeding with bite wounds on their legs and faces sometimes with a torn ear pumping blood or a ripped eye. In the worst cases, a whole flap of skin could be hanging from the dog's side. Small breeds grabbed in the jaws of larger ones often had internal injuries. I cleaned up puncture wounds with antiseptic to prevent infection, bandaged torn ears and admitted others for suturing or treatment for shock. Because most Londoners lived in properties without gardens, they streamed into the parks in good weather to lay out in the sun or picnic. They took their dogs with them and immediately let them off the lead. The result was dozens tearing around the park aggravating each other. Many owners irresponsibly released three or four with no hope of controlling them if there was an emergency, such as a fight. No matter how good a dog's temperament might be, the pack instinct often kicks in if one becomes too excited and barks or jumps on another. Some owners are blissfully under the impression that their dog is impeccably behaved and will cause no problem.

Whilst hurtling around, they commonly cut their paws by stepping on carelessly discarded broken glass and arrived at the hospital with their paw swathed in some form of emergency bandage. I took the dog straight into the consulting room, lifted it onto the table and carefully removed the covering to reveal the cut. It could be tiny or a deep slice with a flap of skin and there could be a little blood seeping out or the wound could be pumping blood. You soon knew how serious it was. Sometimes it involved a torn or cut pad with no blood at all, but enough pain to make the dog limp. The procedure was to fill a kidney dish with diluted Savlon, a much-used antiseptic, and grab a handful of cotton wool to bathe the wound. Once clean, I could assess how deep it was and check whether any glass fragments were still embedded. A cut pad was not a serious injury as they did not bleed profusely or require suturing. I would dress the wound and attempt to put a neat bandage over it until it healed. A badly bleeding wound though, needed a quick bathe, a clean, tight bandage, and a referral to see the vet later.

I always loved bandaging, even though my efforts were often a bit hit and miss. It was always a challenge to bandage up some difficult part of an animal's body and there are set rules and methods. Some require an antiseptic pad or gauze, or cotton wool between the toes, or a support bandage. Ears bleed profusely, particularly if the tip is torn, as the wound will continue to open up and bleed when the animal flicks it through irritation. It is very difficult to put a bandage on successfully, so that it stays on and doesn't slip off. The ear has to be flipped back and a bandage placed right over the dog's head and under the neck. It could turn out to be a mess or a masterpiece, but once finished, I always stood back and admired my handiwork.

*   *   *

Police vehicles blocked off the street and we were almost dazzled by flashing blue lights. The whole street seemed to be full of fire appliances and we picked our way carefully across the fire hoses, strewn like spaghetti across the road. Ten minutes earlier, we had received an urgent call for assistance from the Fire Brigade to attend a major fire in Hackney and I had taken a colleague along for help. It was at times like this that we repaid the Fire Brigade for all the help they gave us. A senior officer appeared out of the blue flashing lights and approached us.

'The whole house is gutted and the owners have been taken to hospital. There are two dogs involved. One is still in the house and will not leave. It attacks us every time we go in. The other is running round in the street somewhere. There he is over there,' he suddenly pointed.

The officer rushed off shouting and we went in search of the loose dog. He appeared round the back of a fire engine, eyes glazed and shaking. He was obviously terrified with all the noise and commotion, but unwilling to leave the familiar environment of the street. He barked at us as we approached and then ran a short distance away. After several attempts to corner him we gave up and decided to concentrate on the one in the house. We hesitantly walked in, our torches giving some scant light. There was the usual smell of smoke, charred wood and water. A firefighter appeared out of the gloom.

'Are you here for the dog?' he asked, 'Well follow me and be very careful as everything is unsafe.'

The floors and walls were all charred and I could still see smoke spiralling and drifting in the torch beam. We tentatively followed to the top of some stairs.

'He's down there in the basement, but he is a nasty bleeder and has refused to have anything to do with us. We need to get down there.'

Two further firemen appeared obviously wishing to see what we intended to do. My colleague returned to the van to get a grasper and while I waited for him, the second dog suddenly trotted into the hallway from outside. He stood glowering at us for a few seconds and then turned to run, but my colleague appeared at that moment. I quickly shouted to him that the dog was heading his way and he managed to rope him as he dashed out the front door. This was a great stroke of luck, as it would save us a lot of time and energy trying to chase round the streets after him. We deposited the poor dog into the van and returned to the basement stairs to retrieve the other.

I led the way slowly down the stairs with a fireman behind shining a powerful torch to light my way. My colleague followed behind him with the other two tagging along at the back. Had there been any spectators to this, I am sure we would have looked rather ludicrous. We all carefully crept down the charred stairs and were rather tense in the eerie atmosphere. Suddenly a snarling brown mongrel appeared at the bottom of the stairs. The impact of his sudden appearance from nowhere made me instinctively flinch and jump back. I cannoned into the man with the torch who fell back onto my colleague. He lost his footing and tripped the following two. The result was a pile of bodies floundering and swearing on the stairs, which soon gave way to hysterical laughter as the comic side to five grown men being spooked by a terrified little dog hit home. By the time everyone had untangled themselves, I had managed to get hold of the dog. Once restrained, he seemed to be relieved to have been rescued, and was soon wagging his tail as we all made a fuss of him. They spent a night at the hospital and were found to have suffered a few patches of singed fur, but no serious ill effects from the smoke or their trauma. The owner was hospitalised for a while, so the dogs were boarded until they could all be reunited in new accommodation.

The most dogs I ever had to help rescue from a fire occurred at a small terraced house, where an old lady lived in poverty with eleven of all shapes and sizes. One of them knocked over an oil stove that was her only source of heating and the whole house went up. When I arrived there were dogs running everywhere. With the help of the assembled men, we managed to round up five in the street and four that were cowering in the garden. Sadly, one had been overcome by smoke and died and we found her little body in the house. The eleventh was nowhere to be seen. There were far too many of them for me to accommodate in my van, so the Police laid on some of theirs and a convoy of vehicles took them back to the hospital to be examined. The poor old lady had survived unscathed and was more concerned about the missing dog than the fact that her house had been gutted and was uninhabitable. Two hours after the incident, I received a call about a dog, found collapsed and salivating, in a doorway a few streets from the fire. Sure enough, it was the missing eleventh dog that had run off in a total panic at the arrival of the Fire Brigade. He was reunited with his nine friends and the owner was delighted when informed of his reappearance. With no house to live in she was unable to take the dogs and was not willing to sign any of them over to the Society for re-homing, so they were all boarded. In the end Social Services managed to persuade her to hand most of them over to the RSPCA, but I believe she did manage to hang on to a couple of them.

* * *

'Thanks for coming down,' said the Sergeant, 'we have been having trouble with this all day. Our dog handlers have been down here, but they haven't been able to catch her. She is extremely nasty and keeps running around and attacking us if we get near. We thought you might have better luck as we don't want to have to shoot her,'

'Well I will have a go, but I cannot promise. I see you have brought plenty of help,' I laughed looking at the two panda cars, a police van, two constables and a policewoman.

'I think they are just here to see the fun rather than help,' he admitted.

Bow Street police had called us early one summer evening to ask if we could assist them in catching a vicious dog that had taken up residence in a scrap yard and wouldn't allow anyone in. As we entered, I was relieved to see that it was a relatively small area, perhaps only an acre. It was filled with stacks of old car bodies, machinery, engines and scrap metal. We had only walked a few yards when I heard a very loud and deep growl to my left. I looked round to see an extremely large, longhaired German Shepherd dog. She was crouching some thirty yards away with her ears flattened in a threatening manner and staring coldly at us.

'We think she has a litter of pups hidden somewhere, but none of us have been brave enough to go searching. Not very friendly as you can see,' remarked the Sergeant.

'I think you are right about the pups as her teats are really swollen and full of milk. Have we any idea where she is from or how she got here?' I asked hopefully.

'The owner of the yard has no idea. She slipped in unnoticed according to him.'

'Are we sure the dog isn't his? I have known them to do this before to get rid of a dog they cannot control.'

'Well we have no way of really knowing,' he said.

'I suppose she thought the place was quiet and had plenty of places to hide the puppies. It must have seemed a good idea to her at the time.'

At this point the dog made a few menacing steps towards us and our brave little group of four police officers and an RSPCA officer stepped back as though one.

'I have to say she is very intimidating,' I commented.

'Well what do you think,' asked the sergeant slightly embarrassed.

'I would say she is definitely protecting her puppies and if I can get to the pups she will probably calm down, but for that I will need some help.'

The Sergeant called over to his two constables: 'You have volunteered to help this gentleman.'

'You have to be joking, Sarge,' exclaimed one!

'Well that will teach you a lesson to tag along when you should have better things to do,' he retorted.

I went to my van, got two graspers and a basket in case I found puppies, and returned to where the two constables stood.

'Right the plan is that you will have a grasper each and stand either side of me and escort me in. If she tries to have a go you can fend her off with these, or better still we might be able to get one of them over her head and restrain her,' I explained.

'Now you are joking,' mumbled one of them.

'Yeh, I wouldn't depend on us if I were you, as dogs frighten me at the best of times,' said the other.

Not feeling very confident, I walked in the direction of where we last saw her with my trusty bodyguards in tow. We hadn't progressed very far when she appeared, growling and barking. I walked towards her with the two officers lagging slightly behind.

'You are supposedly protecting me, you know,' I reminded them.

The dog actually jumped back as we slowly approached, but her courage returned and she made a run at us baring her teeth. One of the police officers to my relief moved alongside me with the grasper outstretched and she ran off behind the jumble of metalwork. I walked in the direction of where she had gone and noticed that she became increasingly agitated and started circling us at a distance. I then faintly heard the unmistakable sounds of young puppies squealing in response to their mum's barks. I headed to the sound while the officers covered my back. I found them in the remains of an old car. There were four and only a day or so old. They were plump and had great little pink noses. Their eyes were totally closed, as like kittens, puppies eyes do not open until they are seven to ten days old. I picked one up and at the sense of my presence they all started squirming and squealing. This immediately alerted mum who instead of being agitated, started sniffing the air with her ears pricked. She was now more concerned about what we were doing to her brood than attacking us. I had all four of them in my hands and I offered them to her. I could see the worry and concern on her face and she stepped slowly towards me, but then her nerve failed and she retreated again. I started talking to her with my arms outstretched with the puppies lying in my hands. I quietly asked the two policemen to back off slightly and leave me with one of the graspers. After five minutes of encouragement, she gave in and came up to check on her offspring. I placed them on the ground and while she gave them a concerned sniff, I managed to get the grasper over her head. She went manic for a couple of minutes, but when she realised she couldn't get away, she calmed down. The Sergeant who had been watching events from a safe distance came over.

'Well done, you made it look easy,' he gushed.

'I presume she is going to Battersea?' I asked.

'I'm afraid so.'

I put the other grasper over her head as well just in case and left my wary bodyguard holding on to her. I closed the basket lid and stood up. The mum was standing a yard away watching the events with a concerned stare. At this point, I made the mistake of turning round to speak to the Sergeant and without warning she chose this moment to launch herself at me.

My two bodyguards, thinking she was now passive, had not been holding the graspers very tightly and she managed to sink her teeth round my skinny calf. She really meant business and would not let go. The two policemen tugged at the graspers to pull her off, but she just held on more tightly and the resulting pain was excruciating.

'Don't pull on those damn things,' I screamed 'you're making her tear my leg to bits.'

I was lying on my side trying to fend the dog off with my other foot. She suddenly let go and was pulled away by the officers. I was left sitting there, clutching my leg and trying not to scream. I could feel blood trickling down and I didn't have the courage to lift my torn trouser leg and view the damage she had caused.

'Christ that hurt. What did you do that for?' I shouted at the dog.

The panting dog stood there staring at me with what I thought was a wicked grin on her face. She had her revenge.

'Are you OK?' asked the Sergeant, who obviously felt he should say something to drown the laughing of his officers who had found the incident more amusing than I had.

'I think so. I'll just go to the van to get something to sedate her with,' I said through gritted teeth. This was just an excuse to hobble off and out of their earshot to have a little scream and to view the wound. She had bitten both sides of my leg quite deeply and my whole leg was now throbbing. It really takes the wind out of you when you are badly bitten. Although a hazard of the job, it didn't happen that often, but when it did, it was a shock. I hobbled back.

'You'll be taking her to Battersea for us I presume,' enquired the Sergeant.

'You must be joking,' I replied, 'I will probably need a lift from you to the hospital.'

'That bad is it?' he asked, slightly put out.

'I'm afraid so.' I lifted my trouser leg so that they could see the bleeding teeth marks and discoloured skin.

I managed to give a sedative injection after a slight struggle and the mum and pups were put in a police van and headed off to Battersea Dogs Home. A police officer kindly drove me in my van to the nearest casualty department. Unfortunately, it was a busy evening there and I had to wait two hours before a Doctor rather unsympathetically stated 'Shame I am not a canine dentist. I could make a perfect set of dentures for that dog from your leg.' I still have a scar from one of her teeth to remind me of the incident. I never heard what happened to the dog and her pups.

* * *

'He's down there, mate. I don't know how you are going to get him out. We have tried, but the mud is too deep,' said the panting and excited man.

I had just arrived on the bank of the River Lee, which runs in a north south direction through the East End of London. It was low tide, the mud banks were exposed, and some ten yards away, stuck up to his chest in the mud, was a longhaired German Shepherd. Why was it always a German Shepherd? It was certainly the most popular dog of the time judging by the amount I came across. He was standing there exhausted, all forlorn and pathetic, coated in evil smelling mud with his head hung low just above the surface. This was going to be a fun way of spending a Sunday afternoon.

Luckily, it was a pleasantly hot and sunny day. I weighed more than the dog, which meant one thing was for sure, if he had sunk that far, I was going to sink even further. So I immediately got on the radio back to base and asked my colleague to summon the Fire Brigade. Within ten minutes, a fire tender came crawling along the road looking for me and I walked into the road to wave them down.

'I'm afraid it is going to be a messy one,' I informed the Officer.

Luckily, everyone appeared to be in a good mood and the crew seemed to relish the idea of mucking about in the mud.

'Get a ladder and some rope,' shouted the Officer and we all trooped down to the river's edge.

One of them decided to test the mud and stepped boldly onto it, only to sink alarmingly up to his thigh, much to the amusement of his colleagues. They pulled him out and decided to lay the ladder across to form a walkway. On seeing it approaching him the dog began to panic, but he was firmly embedded. I was pleased in a way, as it is always embarrassing to see a supposedly trapped animal free itself at the approach of the Fire Brigade. With the ladder in place, a fireman crawled out.

'What happens if he goes for me?' he inquired.

'We will have to try and get a muzzle on him if he does. I can give you this grasper if it is any help,' I said.

'Well at least I can fend him off with it,' he said, 'Chris, come and give me a hand will you.'

Another fireman started crawling along the ladder as back up, and the rest of us watched from the shore. The dog started to struggle again as the first man neared him, but it appeared he wasn't trying to escape, just attempting to get to him to be rescued.

'He's no fool. He has had enough and wants out of there,' laughed one of the assembled firemen.

He continued to try to scramble towards the rescuer, who on reaching the end of the ladder, quietly talked to the dog. He reached out and was soon patting the dog on the head.

'I don't think he is going to be any trouble,' he shouted to us.

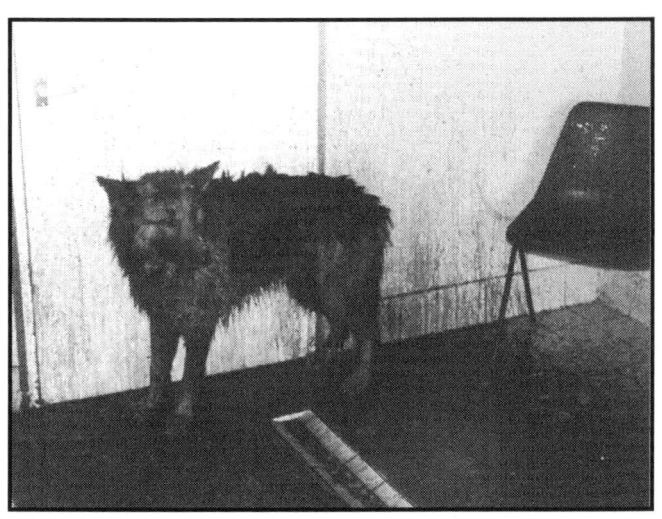

I had never seen a dog covered in so much mud

He managed to get his arm under the body and gave a heave whereupon the dog almost leapt out of the mud into his arms. He tottered back with it in his arms helped by the second man. I met them at the bank and slipped a lead on. They were all plastered in mud. He was wagging his tail at all the attention being given to him. I have never seen a dog so filthy and every square inch of fur was caked in mud. I thanked them for the rescue and opening the back doors, the dog jumped in, where he gave a good shake. The whole of the inside plus all the equipment was covered. I thanked the dog profusely, as I knew I would now be spending a lot of the afternoon cleaning the van. Back at the hospital, I walked him into a small, enclosed yard, which had a tap and hose. My colleague and the duty nurse were also amazed at how filthy he was, but volunteered to give him a bath. They put on long plastic gowns and hosed him down. Every few minutes he would give a tremendous shake plastering the two of them and everything around with mud. Meanwhile I took everything out of the van and started to clean the interior. Luckily, it was a quiet afternoon.

8:

Wildlife Matters

London attracts its fair share of wildlife, due to the extensive areas of available habitat. In the area we covered there were large areas of rough parkland such as Hampstead Heath and Hackney Marshes and dozens of formal parks. All these had ponds or lakes attracting water birds. Railway embankments, tunnels and goods' yards provided acres of suitable land for a variety of wildlife. There were reservoirs, sewage waterbeds, rivers and canals and at the time, huge areas of wasteland in the Docklands and the East End awaiting redevelopment.

The fox is one wild animal that continues to be successful in colonising London. A strong healthy fox is quite a sight with its bushy white tipped black tail and lush fur. Unfortunately, many urban foxes bear no resemblance to their magnificent country cousins and are thin, balding and sickly. Many Londoners welcome and enjoy their company in back gardens and parks, but many others feel they carry and spread disease, are vicious and destructive. They feel that the fact many are unhealthy proves they do not thrive in an urban environment and are a danger to children and other pets. Some of this may be true, but they are probably no more disease ridden or vicious than the rat and there are far more of them in London, but they keep out of sight and therefore out of the mind of the public. Most foxes and rats are there because of the messy habits of the human population. Discarded take-away wrappings, waste food and over-flowing rubbish bins make very easy pickings. With fewer latchkey and stray dogs roaming the streets these days, the fox has no competition or predators to chase them away so their numbers have increased. We received telephone calls from either end of the spectrum. Some people telephoned wanting to know the best way to evict the animals from the neighbourhood either humanely or by any means possible while others wanted advice on how to feed them and encourage them into their gardens. Some threatened that unless we did something to get rid of them they would shoot or poison them and complained that they killed cats or grabbed fish from ponds, which was extremely rare, if it occurred at all.

Their most heinous crime in the eyes of most is the fact that they will kill a group of chickens and only carry one off to eat. It is believed that they get into a state of bloodlust and cannot control themselves. What has to be remembered is that they are wild creatures. Chicken keepers are aware of what they are capable of, so should make sure their chickens are securely confined so that foxes cannot cause this carnage. In the same respect people should also make sure their bins are secured and that they do not discard half-eaten takeaway food. With a little effort on our part, it is possible to live in harmony with local wildlife.

With so many foxes around, there was obviously a time when they got into trouble. Instances of them getting their heads stuck in open tins or plastic bags while scavenging were common. I turned up once to find a fox tearing around and bumping into walls and fences with a tin stuck fast over its head. It was a case of chasing after it with the dog grasper and with thick gloves and a blanket, subduing it so that I could try to pull the tin off its head. They were rarely injured in these incidents so I could just let them go again.

Others got themselves trapped between walls, or fell down into an enclosed space or shut into a building. Some fell sick from the same diseases that dogs come down with or were injured in a road accident. I was often called to poisoned ones where either people had carried out their threat to get rid of them or the fox had accidentally eaten poison destined for rats or plants. I would find the animal prostrate and rigid with its back arched and stiff legs stretched out. Other symptoms were collapse, twitching and staggering depending on which poison they had consumed. Mange and other skin problems were very common in the urban fox because of their poor diet and contact with infected dogs. It was often the case that the foxes I was called to help were too sick to save and many died or had to be put to sleep.

On rare occasions, I was called to collect a litter of cubs left alone after their mother had been killed. Very young cubs, like most young animals are the most appealing things. Any sick or injured fox was returned to the hospital for treatment where there was a special ward for wild animals. If they responded well we would keep them until recovered, then in the early hours of the night return them to the area I had found them. If it required a period of rehabilitation, we would transport them to one of our wildlife centres in the country.

Another unpopular wild animal with many people is the grey squirrel, which flourishes in all the parks and gardens throughout London, and these little creatures fascinate many visitors. Tourists and office workers in central London are always taking dozens of photographs or sharing their lunch with them, but a few people find them unattractive and view them as rats with bushy tails and even the law outcasts them as pests. It was common for me to collect squirrels that had been involved in road accidents or injured by dogs.

Loath them or love them, most Londoners cannot resist feeding them.

I often came across abandoned or sick babies and these were a delight to handle and bottle-feed. The problem with treating and helping these creatures back to health is that because of their illegal immigrant status they cannot be legally returned to the wild. It is an actual offence to let them go. Even though grey squirrels have been resident in the UK for a very long time, they cannot claim asylum status like their human counterparts. Of course being a law abiding responsible person myself, I cannot recall ever releasing one of these terrible creatures!

*   *   *

'The poor little thing is in the side alley round here. I have put a box over him as you said,' explained the concerned householder as she led me round to the side of the house.

'He was covered in flies and looks in a bad way,' continued the woman.

I could see the cardboard box and I walked over to it, knelt down and slowly lifted it. Underneath was quite a large hedgehog. A hedgehog out and about in daylight and in the afternoon sun is not a good sign and the fact that he wasn't curled in a ball was bad news. The poor thing was lying there on his side obviously very ill with his eyes, nostrils, mouth and ears covered in tiny white specks, which were fly eggs. His body was also covered in grey blobs, which were bloated ticks and he was breathing heavily with bubbles issuing from his nose. He was quite limp to pick up and his body was very cold. Basically, he was in a sorry state and dying.

'He is in a very serious condition and past saving I am afraid,' I explained to the finder.

'I thought as much, but I couldn't leave him there suffering could I?' she said sadly.

'No, you have done the right thing. He would have had a painful lingering death.'

'You'll put him out of his misery then?'

'Yes, I'll go back to the van and do that now.'

'Thanks for coming out so quickly. I don't know what I would have done if you were not there to help.'

I carried the prostrate hedgehog back to the van, thinking what a nice, understanding and realistic woman she was. If only everyone we dealt with was like her, the job would be even more rewarding. I took out the first aid box and filled a syringe with the drug we used for putting animals painlessly to sleep. It is an anaesthetic that by injecting an overdose quickly puts the animal under and stops the heart. The hedgehog died peacefully within seconds. People often asked me whether I got upset at having to put animals to sleep. On occasions, I did, but as in this case, the animal I was putting to sleep was usually in agony or beyond recovery, so it eased my conscience to know that I was alleviating pain and suffering. Whenever possible, I preferred to put an animal to sleep on my own as I found it a very personal thing; something I never liked talking about and never liked doing, but unfortunately it came with the job.

Hedgehogs were a regular customer in one form or another. In the spring, we were inundated with calls about ones that had come out of hibernation too early and in the autumn, it was the opposite when callers were worried that they were not big enough to hibernate. In between, we had to contend with those that were sick or injured. The winter was relatively hedgehog free. These little spiny creatures have a large fan base, which is lucky for them, as they do manage to get themselves into trouble and need all the help they can get.

Any found in the open between mid-October and the end of February may well have been disturbed. If it is rolled in a ball, it is probably still slumbering although it is difficult to establish signs of life. Making a new nest undercover somewhere is the best course of action. They spend all summer eating and building up supplies of fat to last them through hibernation and are usually awake from the beginning of March, as this is the beginning of the breeding season and most hoglets are born in April and May. If they produce a litter of young in late summer, it can cause problems. These late babies do not have the time to grow fat enough before winter sets in and tiny ones can be found wandering around, often weak or distressed and these really need to be taken in and fed. It was generally accepted that youngsters should weigh between 500-600 grams before they can be released. Quite often, the spring babies found themselves abandoned when the mother was killed or died through illness and we were called out to collect them. Very young babies are blind and have white spines up to about the age of two weeks and if found it is important to keep them warm. They require bottle or syringe feeding at this young age, which is a specialist job.

As they are mainly nocturnal, many Londoners do not realise that there are thousands of them roaming the gardens, streets and parks of London. People often telephoned surprised at having seen one scurrying around in their garden in the late evening or early morning. Then the owner of the garden immediately inquired about feeding it, worried that the little thing was hungry. At night, they wander their territory in search of food and they are common in urban areas because they love to eat what we eat. They love household scraps and as humans have a habit of discarding food in an untidy way, there is normally plenty of this food source for them to pick over. The old adage of giving them bread and milk is not such a good idea as undiluted milk can give them diarrhoea. They love tin dog food, soft fruit, soaked dog biscuits and chicken carcasses, so do not be surprised to see them hanging around the local take-away.

They are extremely good climbers, which is not generally known and they can get into and out of all sorts of places. Now and again they do come unstuck, fall into sheer sided or deep recesses, and have to be rescued. Finding one abroad in daylight can indicate they are sick or injured. During the summer months, we were often called out to collect sick or injured ones. I would ask callers to place them in a box or container until I could get there. As everyone knows, they have a defence mechanism of curling up in a ball, which makes them very difficult to handle or examine. The spines are incredibly sharp and it is always best to use thick gloves or thick cloth to pick them up. Another trick is to get a piece of cloth large enough to gently roll the animal onto with your foot and then pick up the four corners. A hedgehog that does not roll up when it is touched or hears a noise is usually a very sick creature indeed and the outlook of survival is poor. Examining one that is rolled in a ball is not an easy task. They are extremely strong and trying to force them to open up can injure them. Placing them on a table top and being extremely quiet often prompts them to unravel. Then, grab their hind legs and suspend them over the table so that their front legs touch the table, this usually keeps them busy while they are being examined.

They are always infested with fleas, ticks and lice even when healthy, but if they suffer wounds or become sick the flies soon attack them. It is so sad to see the eyes and nose of these little creatures covered in white eggs or maggots. Sometimes they can become invaded with so many ticks that the blood loss causes severe weakness. The huge bloated grey bumps can easily be seen latched all over the body between the spines and it can take ages to remove them all because the mouth-parts of the tick can be deeply embedded in the skin. Leaving the mouthparts behind can cause infection. Dabbing spirit, ether or chloroform on the ticks first was always a good way of removing them.

Luckily, for hedgehogs, they have few enemies either in the human or animal world and I certainly did not mind coming to their rescue whenever they required it.

Hedgehogs are always covered in ticks and fleas.

*   *   *

'We did as you said, but haven't seen any parent bird in the last couple of hours,' the lady of the house informed me as she led me into a large garden full of shrubbery, where we found her husband sitting in a deck chair; the house was in a leafy part of Hampstead.

'This is my husband,' she announced.

'Good afternoon. We have been keeping watch from a discreet distance, but no luck I am afraid. The babies are still in the box, but we are getting worried now,' he explained.

He got up from the chair and led me over to a large bush at the end of the manicured lawn. Suspended from a branch was a wicker basket. I tipped the basket slightly so that I could see inside and on seeing my head looming over them, four small fledgling birds started gaping and screaming at me. There is something about fledgling birds. Most are ugly, but when you see these enormous yellow mouths upturned at you and their frantic squawking, you have to love them and feel sorry for them. They have this endearing habit of fluttering their wings as they beg for food.

'So you found them on the ground?' I enquired.

'Yes, I do not know how their nest was disturbed, but the remains of it are up there", he pointed. 'I put them in the basket as you suggested and have kept an eye out for the mother, but have not seen any sign of her.'

'And it has been a couple of hours now?' I asked.

'I would say at least that long.'

'OK I think I shall have to remove them as they really need feeding every half an hour or so and they have already missed a few feeds.' I gently lifted the tiny squawking and fluttering creatures into a basket I had with me.

'You're not going to kill them are you,' demanded the wife almost threateningly.

'Of course they're not my dear,' soothed the husband, peering at me imploringly in case that was exactly what I was going to do.

'We have a ward full of them back at the hospital and these will be joining them,' I assured her. Happy with this they escorted me back to my van.

During the fledgling season of spring and early summer the telephone calls to the RSPCA probably increased by fifty percent, as a constant stream of concerned members of the public called in to report finding young birds in trouble. It was a nightmare period, as very few people who telephoned accepted the advice we gave of leaving the birds alone and arguments were rife. Because the well intentioned disturbance of these youngsters was such a problem, the RSPCA and RSPB jointly had a leaflet and poster campaign with the image of a young bird with the words "Leave Them Alone" written above the picture.

Even with constant publicity and advice, the hospital became overrun with fledglings the public had brought in or we had been forced to collect. Very few are genuinely abandoned or lost. Most have fallen out of their nest during exuberant wing stretching and practice flying sessions, when to their surprise they find they have lifted off, only to glide or fall ungracefully to the ground. Some get accidentally pushed out by parents or nest mates, some fall out of their own misfortune and sometimes nests are destroyed. On rare occasions, the parents may be killed.

Maternal or paternal instincts often resulted in people scooping up these birds and taking them home, while the parents would be perched overhead somewhere distraught at what was happening. It is far better to leave them alone, failing that, to put them somewhere safe from marauding cats, children or traffic. Better still, if you can discover the nest they have fallen from, put them back. Another trick is to suspend some kind of container near the nest site in a sheltered spot. A plant hanging basket lined with soft hay and leaves is a perfect nest substitute as it gets them off the ground and gives them a better chance. Failing this any basket, strong cardboard box or plastic container suspended with string or chains will suffice. The parents will soon find them by responding to their calls and continue to feed them. Older youngsters that have virtually all their feathers in place will often immediately jump back out again. This is because they have reached the stage where they need to flex their wing muscles in order to fly. They have been squatting in a nest for weeks with no exercise and therefore have not had the chance to build up muscle strength. There is nothing to do for these birds, as they do not require feeding and left to their own devices will quickly become airborne. Many will be killed during this stage of their development, but this is unfortunately nature's way.

Once they had been brought into us, it was too late to take them back to where they were found. Anyway, the finder would not appreciate the baby bird that they had taken so much trouble to rescue, being abandoned back to where they had found it. It was checked over to see if it had any injuries or ailments. It is pointless trying to hand rear a sickly or injured one with a broken leg or wing and so these were painlessly put to sleep. Those that had a chance were admitted and the bird room would then start to fill with an assortment of tiny creatures at different stages of development. Whenever anyone approached or they heard a noise an array of beaks would open accompanied by a frantic and loud mixture of squawks, all pleading for the same thing: food and lots of it. Hand-rearing them required a lot of patience, time and hard work. It usually got very messy as well. They needed to be kept warm and required feeding at least every hour from dawn until dusk.

Luckily, if they were relatively healthy on arrival, they were easy to feed, as they automatically gape for food and when they felt the food touch their mouth would gulp it down with strangled squawks.

It was essential to establish which species they were so that the bird could be fed the right mixture. Most baby birds, even if they are seedeaters, are fed spiders, insects and grubs by their parents when they are young. Small species such as tits can be difficult to feed as they have such tiny beaks while birds such as crows need food virtually shovelled in. A steady hand is required and an assortment of implements such as tweezers, matchsticks and small spoons. It is difficult to over-feed them, as they normally close their beaks when they feel they have had enough. Sadly, even with all the time, care and attention showered on them, a sizeable percentage would die, probably suffering in the process. It was for this reason that we desperately tried to stop people disturbing them and bringing them into us. It was always upsetting for those looking after the little characters to see them become dull and quiet and then die.

It is, unfortunately, very common for people in London to own parrots and cockatoos which, particularly in the summer, when windows are left open, manage to escape. We would then receive frantic telephone calls from the owner stating that their beloved parrot was sitting in the top of a high tree nearby and could we rescue it. The fact that the parrot was in its natural element, sitting in a tree and was not actually "stuck" ever appeared to register with them. When I pointed this fact out, the owner was not usually that receptive. In fact, the attitude of most parrot owners in this situation was that they expected the Fire

Brigade and us to drop everything and come to the aid of the bird. There was never any thought of them attempting a rescue themselves. I advised the owner to keep calling the bird or to leave its cage below the tree with food in it to try to tempt it back. It was very rare for these methods to work, but it was always worth a try. I was extremely loathe to call out the Fire Brigade to these incidents, as I could not really justify that the bird was "stuck" or even suffering as, after all, the bird was probably gloriously happy at being out and about and enjoying freedom. So many parrots have escaped in London over the decades that many now live wild. Go to many London parks such as Hampstead Heath, Kew Gardens and Richmond Park and you will find flocks of ring-neck parakeets screeching and flying around enjoying themselves.

* * *

'Are you sure this pigeon cannot fly?' I asked

'I am very sure. It's been up there clanking about all morning so it has had plenty of chance if it could. It's been driving me mad, clunk, clunk all over the roof,' stated the lady of the house.

'And you say its leg is stuck in a tin can,' I continued.

'Well I wouldn't have called you if it wasn't. You can see him out of the kitchen window.'

We had received this call an hour earlier and had been a little suspect about attending as it could have been a waste of time. The bird was not confined and was on a roof and had apparently managed to get its leg stuck in a tin can. I went into the kitchen and looked out of the window. Sure enough, on a flat roof at the back, there was a rather confused looking pigeon on his side with a small baked bean tin of the well-known brand attached to its leg. It was always pleasing to attend something different. Although pigeons have an amazing propensity for getting themselves into weird and wonderful predicaments, I had never had to rescue one in this particular situation before.

'I'll get my net from the van as I think that when I get on the roof, he will panic, and try and fly off. I will have to see what happens,' I said. I went and got my net, similar to a fisherman's keep net and, having no ladder with me I dragged a dustbin over to the building wall. I managed to pull myself on to the flat roof and immediately the pigeon took fright. He tried to fly off, but only managed to get six inches off the ground as the weight of the tin can held him down. He continued flapping and disappeared off the edge of the roof. The weight of the tin dropped him to the ground into an alley.

'Great,' I exclaimed and I had to follow, jumping down after him. On the ground, he had nowhere to go and I was able to grab him without the net. On examining him, it was obvious what had happened. Someone had opened the tin with an opener, but not fully and had left a small part of the rim so that the lid was still attached. The tin had been discarded and somehow the pigeon, as only pigeons can do, had trod on it. His weight had caused his leg to slip into the tin. Trying to get his leg out had caused the lid to shut and wedge his foot. By gently pressing the lid down I was able to release him from his bondage and there appeared to be no damage done. I showed the pigeon to the woman who had reported him; assured her that he was OK and then when I was out of sight I released him. He flew off quite happily to find some other scrape to get into.

Ambulance calls to assist pigeons accounted for half our work, particularly at weekends. This is not surprising as there are probably more of them than any other animal or bird in the capital with the exception of the rat. Pigeons are disliked by many people who believe they spread disease and because they create a great deal of mess and damage. Local authorities spend millions trying to eradicate them, protect buildings from them and to clean up after them. Like most birds, they are messy when in large numbers and they can cause some damage when looking for somewhere to roost or nest. I have to admit that I quite like them and have always had a soft spot for them. They are not the brightest animals on the planet and the constant call outs to assist them could be a pain, but to me they were harmless creatures, which had the same rights to a good life as any other creature.

Go to any square, park, train station or large public or office building and you will find a motley collection of feral ones. Inbreeding, poor diet, disease and accident result in pigeons of varying size, colour, health and deformities. There will be some with clubbed feet, missing legs and broken wings; that are blind or have an eye missing; that are limping, or have broken or deformed beaks. There will be some that are fat, thin, have shiny feathers or covered in oil or dirt. The variations are endless. Their life is a constant struggle to survive, but amazingly most will manage to do so even if not healthily. This is mainly thanks to the help of office workers and tourists who find it a pleasing and therapeutic pastime to share their lunch with these creatures. In fact, without the help and encouragement of people they could not survive in the numbers they do. Those birds that have given up the struggle to survive can be seen hunched in doorways, alleys and dark corners waiting to die. Most people will pass them by during their daily rush to lunch, shopping or while heading home after work. Some kind-hearted souls though, found time to telephone and report their predicament.

Ambulance calls to assist sick and injured pigeons accounted for half of our call outs

Although we endeavoured to help as many of them as we could, the time and manpower available restricted what we could achieve, so we tried to convince finders to take the sick or injured pigeon into a local veterinary surgery, bring it to us or at least cover it with a box , but this often fell on deaf ears. Normally I would only attend calls to those that had been confined in some way. On occasions, if I was passing by the address on another call I would look to see if it was still there. To be honest, if I wanted to find sick pigeons I could just go to somewhere like Trafalgar Square and take my pick. You have to be sensible about these things, but emotion can get in the way of sense sometimes.

A pigeon feeding frenzy

At any given time, there are probably hundreds if not thousands in London quietly and sadly dying alone in all kinds of unpleasant circumstances. Most Londoners are blinkered when it comes to them; they are such a part of the London scene that they almost become invisible. In their attempt to thwart them, Local Authorities and landlords could cause them problems and I was continually rescuing trapped pigeons and birds from buildings. Anti-pigeon netting was used as a deterrent and was fitted over buildings to stop them roosting on the window ledges and in recesses, but once in place, the netting was not maintained. Over time holes appeared and they got in only to become trapped. They languished there until they starved to death. Boarded up empty and derelict buildings were broken into by vandals or squatters creating gaps in the windows or doors through which pigeons entered to nest or to roost. Once in, they often couldn't find their way back out, or were boarded in by repairmen.

I often received calls from people claiming to have found baby birds of prey. In every case, these turned out to be baby pigeons, which have to be the ugliest fledgling birds you can ever meet. With large eyes and hooked beaks, it is easy to see how the mistake is made. When very young, they are large, horribly pink, have fat stomachs and have great tufts sprinkled over their bodies, which are the beginnings of feathers. As they grow, skin and feathers grow over and around the beaks to make them look more normal. Pigeons are pretty hopeless when it comes to rearing young. Too stupid and lazy to build nests, they lay eggs anywhere they see fit. This could be a window ledge, the top of a wall, a roof, a recess on a statue, anywhere they can find a relatively sheltered place. The surface doesn't even have to be flat and many eggs will just roll off and smash. The same often happens to the unfortunate babies, so in breeding season I was called to lost and abandoned ones left gasping for life on the pavement. Because of their grotesque looks, a person tended to shy away from them, which was a shame. They do not have the same endearing features as most baby animals.

Feeding pigeons has been a favourite pastime of the Londoner and the tourist for countless years and when I drive past or wander through Trafalgar Square now, it is with great regret that I cannot see the throngs of children and adults shrieking as they are mobbed by clouds of pigeons taking food from their outstretched hands. The decision to eradicate them from the Square and other central London areas seems so unfair when humans are making far more mess of the city than the poor old pigeons ever did.

A relatively quiet weekend could often be shattered by a homing pigeon race. Having devoted so much time and energy rearing and caring for the birds, I cannot understand why anyone would want to release hundreds or even thousands of them into the countryside. Most of the races were completed with only a few birds going missing along the way, but if bad weather in the form of high winds or heavy rain intervened, then it could cause chaos to the race and aggravation for us.

The sport or hobby of racing pigeons has a very large following, the season is from May to September, and all birds have to be registered with the governing body of the sport: the Homing Union. At the time, all birds wore a band on their leg with their registration number stamped on it, but no owner contact details. They are released en masse with the races covering anything from sixty to six hundred miles and the birds are individually timed as they arrive back at their lofts. Many of these races involve 'young birds' or pigeons that have been hatched that year. These might have very little experience or were 'untried' in races and many did not share the same enthusiasm for racing as their owners. If bad weather hits during a race, birds can be blown off course, and be disorientated or become waterlogged and exhausted; they are then forced to land and take refuge. Being used to human handling and company, they are quite friendly and not averse to trying to take up residence and begging for food wherever they happen to make landfall. When the race happened to be near London, they would appear all over the area and were often not welcomed by residents already exasperated with the local pigeon population.

Every year many turned up lost or injured because of this hobby and at weekends, we bore the brunt of calls from the public. The first we knew of a race having taken place was when people started telephoning reporting exhausted pigeons, with rings on their legs, found confused and tame, on their windowsills, at their back doors or on their bird table, looking for food and hospitality. They would notice the metal and plastic rings on their legs and immediately believe they were valuable and required reporting to an authority. As most people didn't have a clue who the governing authority was, they telephoned us for advice.

If injured or obviously sick, we asked the finder to bring it in to us or take it to a local vet. If they refused, we would go and collect it and then immediately had a problem. If it had a damaged or broken wing or leg, we knew the owner might not be that interested in having it back and if we treated the bird, we then had the problem of finding a suitable home for it. If it was not injured, we tried to convince the caller to ignore the bird, shoo it away and definitely not feed it. Human nature being what it is, in regard to pathetic looking animals, this advice was normally ignored, and then the caller found the pigeon wanted to move in with them. When someone contacted us reporting a racing pigeon I advised them to catch hold of the bird and read the registration number on the band. I then gave them the telephone number of the Royal National Homing Union so that the owner could be contacted. Of course, most people did not like this idea. The best solution all round, was to ignore the bird completely, forcing it to fend for itself or hopefully find its own way home.

*   *   *

'There it is up there,' said a police officer pointing up to the roof of a terraced house.

'How are we going to get it then?' asked another.

At this point, a police van came along the street with a loud hailer.

'Would residents please note that there is a dangerous animal on the loose and you are advised to stay indoors and make sure all windows and doors are shut and locked. Please avoid going outside,' came the announcement.

'Yes indeed. What are we going do,' I inquired of my friend, Tony, as I turned to him.

Sitting on a chimney stack, some thirty feet above us, was a large agitated Rhesus monkey. These monkeys hail from Asia and apart from being very strong also have very large teeth. Tony was the deputy manager of the RSPCA Airport Animal Hostel and an ex-member of the night emergency staff. We were standing some four hundred yards from the Hostel outside houses along the Bath Road, a street that runs parallel to the main runway at Heathrow Airport.

In between my night shifts, I used to lodge with my friends Tony and his wife Marion in their bungalow beside the Hostel. The bungalow had the distinction of being the only residential building on the airport and it had quite a large low walled garden from which we had a close view of aircraft landing and taking off. It was from here that I watched Concorde take off for the first time. An hour earlier, Tony had rudely awoken me from my slumbers following a night shift, asking if I fancied helping him catch an escaped monkey. Tony and I had roared off in the Hostel van to join staff already searching. The Police had been informed and eventually turned up in force. The monkey had escaped from an airline van that was delivering a shipment of them to the Hostel and had made the most of his escape by climbing over the perimeter fence, running across the road, jumping in and out of a few trees and eventually "holing up" on the roof of one of the houses opposite. He gazed down at us, and all the activity, with both interest and agitation and then scampered further along the row of houses.

Every time he moved, we all jumped into our vehicles and followed him. On a couple of occasions, he ran out of roofs to clamber across and made his way to the ground. We jumped out of our vehicles, armed with nets, but it was futile. All kinds of tactics were used, including copious amounts of food strewn around for him. There was really no hope of cornering or netting him, as he was far too intelligent, quick and nimble to fall for any tricks. All we could do was follow and hope. This went on for a couple of hours. By this time, we were over a mile from the airport. He did himself no favours on a couple of occasions, by biting one foolish soul who tried to grab him and then chasing a child in a garden. The Police were becoming as agitated as the monkey and they feared for public safety and possible press and media reaction. Eventually, the Police suggested the inevitable; they wanted to shoot the monkey and end the chase. Unfortunately, this was in the days before dart guns were in general use. We were not keen on the idea, but had no real say in the matter. We continued to follow the monkey until Police marksmen arrived on the scene. Announcements by loud hailer cleared the area of spectators and we witnessed the sad sight of the monkey being shot.

Although I witnessed many sad and tragic scenes at the Hostel, which tainted my impression of zoos and the pet trade, I have mainly happy memories of the establishment and great respect for its female staff who worked so hard to feed, water and aid all the poor animals that passed through its doors. The Hostel had been specially designed and built rather unimaginatively in the form of an aircraft hangar beside the old A4 Bath Road. It had opened in 1952 with the purpose of attempting to alleviate the suffering of animals consigned by air. With the onset of the new jet age and pressurised cargo holds, animal dealers and pet owners were now sending animals by air rather than by sea, as it was obviously much quicker.

The Hostel consisted of a huge open hanger, with three rooms down one side, which had large pens and cages on wheels that could accommodate a variety of animals. Along the other side was a line of small rooms for birds and at the end, a staff room with facilities for the 12 girls who worked there day and night. Attached to the hanger on one side was a grass walled paddock and on the other, an area of kennels and a cattery. To the front was the reception, offices, vets room and sickbay. To this day, I can still hear and smell the place. When I walked in my nostrils were assaulted with all the exotic smells of a farm and zoo concentrated into a space a quarter of the size of a football pitch. The smell of damp straw, of pungent urine and droppings, the aroma of rotting fruit and seeds; the barking of dogs, the raucous cries of parrots, the odd roar of a big cat.

At that time, there was no restriction at all, on what animals could be kept as pets. Anyone could keep a lion or monkey in a flat. Also zoos and the pet trade were still continually stocking up on animals caught in the wild rather than breeding them, and so there were literally thousands of exotic animals passing through the airport each day. Add to this all the domestic pets flying all over the world, there was not an hour, day or night, when airline vans were not pulling up outside and opening the rear doors to disgorge every species of animal imaginable. It was common to see baby elephants, big cats, bears, hundreds of monkeys and baboons heading for research, parrots, and finches by the thousand, snakes, crocodiles, otters, hundreds of thousands of tropical fish and thousands of day old chicks twittering away. By lodging next door, I had special access and so many chances to see, experience and enjoy all the creatures that passed through. For me it was like paradise and so exciting. I still remember those days where one minute I would be sitting with Tony and his wife Marion watching television in their lounge and the next minute hurrying over to the hostel following a telephone call from the girls to Tony regarding some problem. Then I would suddenly be helping to get a fractious leopard or bear out of a box or catch a group of monkeys to re-crate them; sometimes to release a consignment of parrots or flamingos. You just never knew what was going to happen next.

I was lucky enough one evening to help bottle feed a baby elephant. I had never touched or been close to an elephant before and to be kneeling next to a tiny elephant, to be touching the rough skin and hair, to be gazed at by its tiny bright eyes, to smell it and watch, as it messily guzzled down pints of warm milk was heaven. On another occasion, I was around to help release a consignment of young otters from Asia into a large pen. Otters are one of my many favourite creatures. They were all tame and I sat on the straw covered floor for over an hour while they chewed on my shoes and trousers, jumped all over me and tried to playfully nip my fingers.

Over the eight years or so that I had access to the Hostel, I must have come across every species of animal there was to see and thoroughly enjoyed myself. Unfortunately a sizeable percentage of animal shipments suffered death and suffering at the hands of animal dealers who tried to cut freight charges by housing the animals in small unsuitable crates and airlines who were incapable of enforcing their own regulations. Of the million odd animals that passed through the Hostel annually, they reckoned they had over 13,000 mammals, birds and reptiles plus staggering numbers of tropical and marine fish and day old chicks dead on arrival. Many shipments were passing through to be flown on to other countries during which time more would die.

In 1981, the RSPCA Airport Hostel closed its doors having been replaced by the Quarantine Station that is there today. Its dedicated staff had looked after some 20 million animals since it opened in 1952. They had sweated, risked injury and illness from catching zoonotic diseases. They had nursed, fed, removed rotting evil smelling bedding and carcasses and saved many thousands of lives, but their achievements are long forgotten and I doubt very few people know that there had been such a remarkable place on the site. The building remained derelict for quite a long time before being demolished.

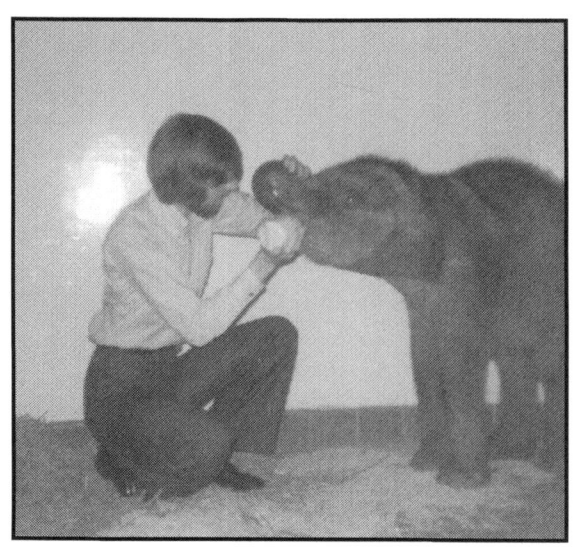

I could not believe I was lucky enough to be bottle feeding a baby elephant

I was sitting in a cage full of my favourite animals - I thought I was in heaven

9:

People and Places

I was sitting in my van outside a house in Furrow Lane, Homerton, in the East End, waiting for a Social Worker to arrive. The windows of the house were mainly broken and had been roughly covered with a patchwork of ill-fitting wood. The front door was rotting and bare of paint. We had been summoned by Hackney Social Services to help an old lady, who was sharing her two-room ground floor flat with fifteen or so stray cats of varying states of ill health. They had explained that the she had been living there with an old man to whom she was not married. He had recently died and had been dead for four days when a Salvation Army officer found him on his bed. When asked why she had not done anything about her companion dying, she explained that the two of them had fallen out and hadn't been speaking to each other for a long time. She had not thought to check why he had not stirred from his bed for several days. The house was in a real state and she had no money. Social Services wanted to remove the cats and try to clean the place up for her.

The door of the house suddenly opened and a small lady with long, lank hair and dressed only in a shabby, short-sleeved summer dress hobbled over to the van. It was a cold November day, but she appeared not to notice. I got out and said good morning.

'You the man for the cats?' she asked abruptly.

'I am,' I replied.

'Eh?'

'I said, I am,' I repeated.

'D'you want to come in and see them? Lively cats they are.'

'Perhaps we should wait for Mr Harris, the Social Worker to come,' I suggested

'Eh?'

'I said Mr Harris is coming soon and we should wait for him.'

'Mr Harris coming too is he. He's a nice man. D'you want to see my cats?'

She went back into the house leaving me rather confused outside. I could see this was going to be one of those days and I was praying for Mr Harris to turn up. A few moments later, she appeared carrying a large struggling white cat.

'This is Whitey,' she exclaimed as she tried to keep hold of the hissing and wriggling cat. Whitey suddenly wrenched himself free and disappeared up the street. She rubbed her scratched bleeding arms and tottered back inside the house only to reappear clutching another malevolent looking, one eyed cat.

'This is Blackie. He's only got one eye.'

'So I see. He's very nice, but don't you think we ought to put him back inside before....' Blackie, like Whitey before him, launched himself from her arms and disappeared up the street. I looked despairingly after him and started to believe that the old lady might have some method in her madness. If Mr Harris did not arrive soon, there would be no cats left to take away. Luckily, a smartly dressed man turned the corner of the street and approached us.

'I see you have already met our Hilda. Hello, I'm Mr Harris from Social Service,' he announced cheerfully.

'I'm afraid we have lost a couple of cats already.'

'You are a naughty girl Hilda. I told you not to let them out, didn't I?'

'Eh?'

'She's a bit hard of hearing,' stated Mr Harris 'or she only tends to hear what she wants to hear, if you know what I mean.'

'So I gathered,' I said, having already guessed that this might be the case.

'Let's go in shall we", said Mr Harris leading the way through the front door. 'Be prepared.'

As we entered a room off the hallway, there was a sound of loud crashing as the darkened room erupted in cats leaping in all directions.

'They are a trifle wild,' commented Mr Harris with some understatement.

It was several seconds before my eyes became accustomed to the darkness of the room. When I could vaguely see, I was both stunned and appalled. If there was ever a definition of squalor, then this room was it. The room was dark as the windows were boarded up and light only leaked through gaps and cracks in the boards.

'Hilda hasn't had any electricity or heating for years and her only water supply is a tap in the yard outside,' Mr Harris informed me sadly.

The room was damp and cold with fungus growing on the walls. In one corner, a mattress was propped up on stacks of newspaper. There was an assortment of broken furniture and a gas stove. It was difficult to move round as the floor was littered ankle deep with rubbish. An alcove off the main room contained another bed of sorts where I was informed Hilda's companion had quietly died without notice. Every surface was covered in a thick layer of greasy grime, the consistency of congealed fat in a pan. It was horrible to touch anything, so I tried not to. There was no wallpaper and plaster was hanging from the ceiling. This is how Hilda had been living for years, before being discovered by the Salvation Army.

'Pretty bad, eh?' enquired Mr Harris, as he noticed the grimace on my face. I was realising that Mr Harris had a knack of understatement, probably because of all the sights he must have come across.

'How on earth did they survive in here?' I exclaimed.

'Well, she has been living here as far back as we can discover and the local shopkeepers have been giving them food supplies. It is unbelievable, but neither has been claiming their pensions. They didn't know or understand they could and basically had disappeared off the records.'

'What's that?' shouted Hilda who had been standing impassively in the middle of the room trying to follow our conversation.

'I was saying you didn't know about claiming your pension,' shouted Mr Harris.

'Pension - don't need no pension,' mumbled Hilda.

It took about twenty minutes to explain to her that we had to take her cats away. Because of her deafness, she would put her face two inches from mine and stare intently at me with her misted eyes, trying to catch each word I said, only to say "eh?" to each of my statements. Eventually she agreed that it was not feasible for her to look after the cats properly and she wouldn't be able to take them with her when she was found new accommodation. She also said she would allow Social Services to clean up her flat. I think she only agreed to all this as she was fed up with talking to us.

Armed with a torch I searched for any sign of the cats, which by now had all secreted themselves out of sight amongst the debris of the room. A three hour game of hide and seek then ensued. I moved round the room tentatively and half-heartedly moving furniture and junk, not wishing to look at what I might find. I had to steel myself to look under the beds and left that job until the very end. At one point, several of the cats made a collective assault on the window, knocking the boards aside and disappearing. Mr Harris then volunteered to guard the window but I did not ask what he intended to do if anymore made a rush to escape through it.

(Photo: Help the Aged/Salvation Army).

Hilda only added to the frustration and confusion by her attempts to help. She kept appearing with a struggling cat clutched to her bosom and while avoiding the lashing legs and claws would tell me its name. I would grab it by the scruff of the neck from her and bundle it into a basket, getting badly scratched and bitten in the process. As soon as I turned my back, she would be opening the basket and peering up at me informing me yet again of its name. I then realised she was not as silly as she pretended to be and it was all a subterfuge to stop me taking them. Eventually I managed to get seven cats into baskets and I placed them in the back of the van away from the attentions of Hilda, who was unsure or unwilling to testify to how many cats she looked after, but we estimated it at around twenty. I said I would return at a later date to try to catch the others.

Before departing, I asked Mr Harris what was going to happen to her. Although the Council wanted to find better housing, it was going to be difficult and could take months. In the meantime, they felt there was little they could do. They had glazed the windows before and gangs of vandals, who victimised her, had soon broken these again. No home help would consider entering the property in the state it was in and she was incapable of looking after herself properly. The only glint of hope on the horizon was that a local charity and the Salvation Army were joining forces to clean her place up and try to lay on electricity and heating. I got into my van feeling dirty, uncomfortable and extremely depressed.

I returned to see her a few days later, but she had once again cunningly let all the cats out. The third and last time I visited, I noticed that her windows had been glazed and apparently, someone was collecting her pension. There were no cats to be seen so I decided to give up on the operation. She had won and kept her remaining cats and I wasn't that displeased as they were semi-wild and probably had a pretty good life with her. I gave her a final goodbye and she peered up at me and then disappeared into the cold and damp of her house and her apparent contentment with her lot in life.

A year later, I was enjoying an evening drink in a pub when a Salvation Army lady came in selling the War Cry magazine. As she walked past I happened to spot a familiar face on the front cover and I bought one. Amazingly, it was a front-page story relating to Hilda, and the poverty she had been living in and how she had been finally re-housed. It was terrible to think that she had to wait for so long to be rescued from her slum. I often wonder what her fate would have been if the Salvation Army had not come to her aid.

*   *   *

Local Council Social workers were always contacting us about elderly owners who could not cope with their pets or who had been taken into hospital and their pets required emergency boarding. Unfortunately, many of these people lived in very deprived conditions and were often neglected by society and officialdom. Witnessing the starkness, loneliness, poverty and the often disgusting deprivation they lived in was soul destroying. I came away feeling unclean, saddened and frustrated at not being able to do something more to help them. It was a real culture shock for a young man like me to see how these elderly people lived and survived.

When an aged owner or Social Services contacted us about a pet requiring treatment I attended and took it to the nearest RSPCA vet and once treated returned the animal with the appropriate drugs. For many, their pets were their only company and friends and my visits were often a highlight as it was someone new to talk to.

I always remember a cheerful old lady named Mrs Downs who suffered from arthritis, but was quite content in her first floor flat with her faithful feathered friend Joey the budgie. She had the closest relationship I think you could have with a budgie. The bird was everything to her. It talked and sang to her and would sit on her shoulder while she watched television and even drank tea from her cup. I would often have to call round when it needed its claws clipped or beak trimmed. On this occasion, he had something more serious wrong with him. She greeted me in her normal cheerful way and she huffed and puffed her way up the stairs to her flat.

'It's my heart dear. Doesn't do me any good these stairs,' she wheezed.

The offer of the obligatory cup of tea was accepted, as a refusal would have offended her. We sat passing the time of day for a while as I could see she was upset. She finally brought the conversation round to her beloved Joey.

'Where's that Joey,' she shouted. Joey, who was normally flying like a mad thing round the room, was hunched on top of the sideboard and not looking at all well. 'He's developed a lump on his tummy and I'm quite worried as it's turned nasty.'

I got up and took a close look at him and he just sat all fluffed up and still at my approach. I could immediately see a large red raw lump protruding from under his chest feathers. Mrs Downs remained seated in her chair and I turned and explained that it did look serious, as she had guessed. I gently put him in a small box that I had brought and he did not struggle.

I drove back to the clinic, where the vet confirmed that it was an inoperable cancerous growth and poor Joey would have to be put to sleep. I could not bear to tell her the bad news over the telephone so I drove back to her flat, as I knew that it might be too much for her to bear. I broke the news and she stared at me for a few moments before bursting into tears. She half fainted into a chair and I began to get worried in case her heart gave out. This time I made her a cup of tea and between sobs, she reminisced about Joey. She told me that the decision to have him put to sleep was the biggest of her life. Having assured her that it was the fairest thing to do for him, she gave permission. I promised her that I would do my best to find her a replacement if that was what she wanted. As I left, I saw her walk over to the empty cage and start sobbing again.

I tried for several weeks to find a similar budgie without success. Mrs Downs was telephoning the clinic almost daily distraught at her loss and asking for a Joey look-alike. Finally, one day I collected a stray budgie that bore a remarkable resemblance to him. I telephoned Mrs Downs who got quite emotional and simply said 'it was meant to be.'

I took it straight round to her. She was standing by her front door talking to a neighbour. On seeing the budgie, her face quite literally lit up. She could not stop talking as she climbed the stairs quicker than I had ever seen her do. She had Joey's old cage all cleaned up and ready and waiting. I released the budgie into the cage where it fluttered around for a while before settling on a perch. The new budgie would not have the same party tricks as Joey, but I was sure that she would be spending many pleasurable hours taming the bird and teaching him new tricks. She was almost sobbing with pleasure at having a new flat mate and it was wonderful to witness her joy.

*   *   *

Another old lady who comes to mind was Mrs Edwards who lived in a ghastly nineteenth century tenement block called Farringdon Buildings in the Farringdon Road. To get to her flat I had to walk up a narrow unlit stairway with graffiti plastered over the walls and the smell of urine and alcohol. The corridor was just as badly lit and I remembered that the first time I had visited her I had to use a torch to see the flat numbers. In the semi-darkness, I knocked on her door. Mrs Edwards was a tiny, frail lady who, like most of the elderly people I visited had accepted her lot in life and made do. I could hear her awful chesty breathing as she shuffled along the hallway towards the door.

'Who's there?' I heard a timorous voice call.

'John from the RSPCA,' I answered.

'OK luv. Shan't be a moment.'

I could hear the usual pandemonium from inside as Judy her Jack Russell, and Fluffy her cat, started tearing around at the excitement of someone visiting. Her dog and cat were both characters, but did not get on too well. When I entered, Judy got so excited that she tore around the tiny flat, chasing Fluffy who jumped onto the windowsill knocking everything over, and then dived under a chair with Judy in hot pursuit. It was the same routine every time.

Every year the Nuns from a local convent arranged a holiday for her and the RSPCA boarded her pets. I would come along and collect the animals. On this occasion, she was very excited as she was off to Lourdes to seek a cure for her bad breathing and chest problems. As always, I had great difficulty getting Fluffy into a basket as Judy interfered by barking and trying to grab her. It was always pretty dark in the flat as there was only one small window overlooking a brick wall and Mrs Edwards did not like to have lights on, as she could not afford the electricity. Once the animals were sorted, I spent a few minutes listening to her excited description of the adventure she was about to have and I left. At least she managed to escape her prison once a year unlike many elderly people I knew. She would always thrust a small donation in my hand and we would act out our normal routine of me refusing it because she could not afford it and her being affronted until I accepted it. She was from a generation where it was a principle to try to pay her way and not accept charity. A week later, I was back. Mrs Edwards was beaming and excited at having her two companions back safe and was full of her adventure at Lourdes. Judy was let off the lead, Fluffy let out of her basket, pandemonium broke out and everything was back to normal for another year.

*   *   *

I had received an urgent call over the radio and I was speeding towards City Road at the Angel Islington, a busy crossroads. A horse had apparently fallen into the basement well of a building. These wells are a lower ground floor area in front of terraced houses, which in the old days had a stone staircase down to a tradesman entrance and allowed light into the basement. Most had iron railings protecting them and these days are used for access to a flat.

Animals of all kinds used to fall into, or hide after accidents in these areas, particularly foxes and cats. As I neared the address, I wondered how on earth a horse had fallen into one, particularly as there were very few horses left in this part of London. When I arrived, I saw two fire tenders with blue lights flashing and traffic jams in all directions. In amongst all this was a dishevelled old man attempting to hang onto a terrified horse. I immediately recognised him. His name was Mr Farris and he was from another era: one of the last true rag and bone men who still plied his trade with a horse and cart.

He was a familiar sight in the Islington area, plodding round on his cart with his old Jack Russell sitting next to him. I had several dealings with him in the past and knew him to be a cantankerous old man. He shunned help and did not speak to anyone unless he had no choice. He never said thank you and was quite miserable, but for all this, I did like him. There was something about him that I admired as he tried to continue his age old trade in the heavy traffic. He was of course a bit of a menace and a danger to himself, the horse and the public. He was part of a dying breed, which was soon to disappear from the scene forever and become part of history.

'We have him out as you can see,' stated the approaching fireman, 'the old man is a real so and so. He didn't even thank us.'

I had to smile. 'I know. He never does. How did the horse get down there?'

'Apparently the traffic frightened the horse and it bolted, reared up and toppled down into it. Well, we are done so it's over to you now. We cannot see any obvious injuries. Good luck.' With that, the Fire Brigade roared off leaving me to try to sort out Mr Farris, who was trying to placate his wild-eyed horse.

'Is everything OK Mr Farris?'

'He's orright. Just frightened,' he growled.

'No injuries then. He's got a cut there, look,' I said as I pointed to the horse's front leg.

'He's orright I tell you,' he shouted.

'Well I would get it checked at our clinic sometime soon, just to be on the safe side if I was you.'

This he apparently did, but a couple of months later I was called to his house and yard, which he shared with his long suffering Jack Russell, predictably named Jack, and Jessie his cat. It was a ramshackle place situated in a mews behind the Angel Islington. At one time all these little streets would have been full of stabled horses, but most were now being turned into upmarket little residences and boutiques. It was just round the corner from Camden Passage, a trendy street of antique shops. I could envisage that it would not be too long before he was forced to vacate his property, which would be renovated leaving no trace of him, his animals or his old livelihood. Neighbours would probably not rue his departure. I found him leaning against the stable door, wheezing and coughing.

'What can we do for you then, Mr Farris?'

'It's me animals.'

'What is wrong with them?'

'Nuthin'. It's me who's bleedin' ill. Should have gone into hospital yesterday, but there's no one to look after 'em.'

He must have been poorly to actually ask for help. He did look ill. He was swaying and bringing up blood, which he wiped away with a rag.

'What's wrong with you?'

'Got an ulcer.'

I stepped into the stable. His horse was always well cared for and had an extremely mild temperament after years of plodding round the local streets. I noticed his wound had healed nicely. His black and white cat appeared and walked up to the horse, its tail held high. The horse nuzzled Jessie, who immediately started purring. Jack, probably jealous and not wanting to be left out also wandered up making Jessie back off slightly. It was such a lovely sight to see them all together.

'I see you have still got your cat,'

'Yeh, he loves the horse. Great friends they are, but ol' Jack don't get on too well with the cat. Always chasing him, given the chance,' He started coughing violently and collapsed into an old chair. He was coughing up a lot of blood and I was very concerned.

'What hospital are you going into, Mr Farris?' I enquired.

'Don't like hospitals. Should have been in yesterday, but I can't leave the animals,'

'Well I can take Jack and Jessie now, but the horse will take a little more arranging. Is there anyone who can feed him?'

'Don't know anyone. I can't leave 'em if you can't help,'

'Don't worry. I'll sort something out, but first we need to get you attended to,'

I eventually discovered which hospital he was due to be admitted into and I telephoned them. I asked if they could send an ambulance to collect him, but was told that as he should have arrived the day before they did not have a bed for him now. They were rather unsympathetic about his problems and said it was his fault if he insisted on putting his animals before his own health. The hospital suggested I contact his doctor, so I called him. I got a similar response so getting rather exasperated I dialled 999 instead and made it an emergency. An ambulance duly arrived and Mr Farris grudgingly left his beloved animals, after I assured him they would be looked after.

Having fed the horse, I took Jack and Jessie to one of the animal homes for emergency boarding and arranged for our horsebox to collect the horse the next day. Mr Farris had his operation and after a couple of months was fit enough to have his animals returned. It was quite a reunion. A week later I saw him on his cart plodding along, business as usual and back to his old gruff ways.

*   *   *

The days of Mr Farris and London's rag and bone men have long gone. It is amazing how the face and atmosphere of London has changed in the last 30-40 years particularly in the East End. I have to admit that I do not like modern London and avoid the place as much as possible. I loved working there during the 1970's and I believe this was the last decade that the city retained its old character, style and magic. Perhaps nostalgia has clouded my memories, but London now, like so many cities around the world has lost its identity. All cities are starting to look the same: just high-rise glass buildings. London for me has lost most of its interesting landmarks that gave it its character and individuality. I always felt lucky that I had a job that allowed me to be out and about most of the time meeting people and visiting most of the colourful parts.

There were so many fascinating places to enjoy and many true East Enders: the last members of the blitz generation, to meet and interact with. Agreed, there was still a lot of grime, poverty and decay existing, but back in the early seventies, many of the Docks were still in full swing, along with the famous markets and the Thames remained busy with barges and boats. The sights were not so overrun with tourists and the traffic was less heavy, making driving less stressful. The streets and housing estates felt less threatening and safe to wander round in the dead of night, which I was often called upon to do.

Old World War Two bombsites still littered the East End awaiting overdue re-development. These were large areas of wasteland strewn with building rubble and fenced with corrugated iron. These undisturbed areas became small natural reserves where nature went mad and local children prised open the iron panels to get in and play. No adventure playground could have been designed better. A variety of animals, birds and plants took up residence and these included thousands of stray cats.

In some areas there were dozens of streets of fencing, derelict buildings and small enclaves of prefabricated houses, commonly called prefabs. These one-storey buildings were built soon after the war as temporary accommodation for all the local residents bombed out of their homes. Designed to last ten years until the residents could be relocated, many remained thirty years later. These little communities with their friendly, mainly elderly residents and their neat little fenced gardens are long gone. Many were built on small pillars lifting them about eighteen inches off the ground. The owners placed chicken wire or boards all-round the house to cover the gap to try to stop litter, rats and cats from getting under their homes. Unfortunately, over time, holes or gaps appeared, and cats would get under in search of food or warmth, particularly when they were sick and got themselves trapped.

I walked up to the prefab through a small neat garden, knocked on the door and a middle-aged housewife answered.

'I've come about the cat'.

'Thank goodness. I have been putting food under the house for the last three days, which it eats, but it doesn't seem to want to leave'.

'Have you actually seen the cat?' I asked, as I was worried it might be a neighbour's cat just wandering in every day to eat the free food.

'Oh yes 'e's under there alright. It hides right in the middle and last night my husband shone a torch under there and we saw the cat's eyes staring back'.

'He eats the food you leave for him you say?'

'Sure does. It's not a nuisance or anything, but I don't want it to die under there and cause a smell'.

I got my torch from the van and on my hands and knees shone it under the house. I could not locate the cat so I moved position and had another look. I repeated this all round the house while the housewife followed me. I was still unable to pinpoint it as the house was supported on twenty or so pillars and there was a lot of rubbish behind which it could hide.

'Are you sure it is still under here?'

'Oh yes. It can't get out because of the chicken wire all round'.

'How did it get under here then?'

'My kids keep pulling the wire off, but my husband went round repairing it so the cat wouldn't escape before you came'.

The gap under the prefab was only twelve inches or so and a tight fit for me to crawl under. I persevered with my torch and finally spotted two eyes staring back at me.

'I've found him,' I said to the woman as she appeared with a cup of tea for me.

I gave some thought as to how I was going to capture him and eventually decided to put my extension rods together to form a rod some twelve feet long, which I could push under the house. These rods were similar to those used by chimney sweeps and to push down drains and the problem with them was that they become cumbersome and bendy. I pulled the protective wire mesh away from one side of the house. My plan was to try to frighten him out by prodding and poking the rod about towards him. After fifteen minutes, my endeavours were proving to be useless as he kept backing away from the rod and hiding behind the pillars and made no attempt to escape. I couldn't understand why he liked it under there so much unless he was sick or injured. I gave up on this idea and made the decision that I had been trying to put off and that was to crawl underneath. I did not relish the thought of dragging myself crocodile fashion through all the litter and debris, as you never knew what you might find.

'I am going to have to crawl underneath after it', I announced.

'Rather you than me luv. You must love animals to do that'.

'If the cat should rush out while I'm under there can you let me know which direction he goes?'

'Course I can luv'.

Pushing my torch and grasper in front of me I pulled myself towards the last place I had sighted the cat. I was soon sweating and covered in dust and cobwebs. The two eyes watched my approach nervously and he kept turning his head looking for an escape route. I was within six feet or so of him when he bolted, but I could see all was not right with him. I dragged myself back out and when I re-appeared covered in dust, cobwebs and spiders I must have looked like some apparition rising from the dead.

'It's over there luv in the vege patch in the corner. It was dragging itself and looks really bad'.

I thanked her and slowly and quietly approached the thick growth of potatoes, cabbage and beans, which again made it difficult to spot him. I used the end of the grasper to gently search the undergrowth and suddenly a large tabby cat exited the vegetable patch at remarkably high speed considering his hindquarters were useless and he was dragging himself by his front legs. I intercepted him half way back to the house where he rolled on his side and attacked the grasper I was trying to get over his head. He fought the rope with teeth and claws and was obviously a feral cat. I could see that apart from suffering from a possible broken pelvis or back he had severe cat flu as well. After a terrific struggle, I managed to get hold of him and then had to use all my effort to get him into a basket. Their strength even when badly injured is phenomenal.

'He's badly hurt isn't he?'

'I'm afraid so'.

'Lucky I called you out then, eh?'

'Yes, thanks for that'.

'No problem. As I said I didn't want it dying under there and causing a smell'.

The cat's pelvis and spine was completely smashed probably caused by a lorry running right over the poor thing so all that I could do was to put him to sleep.

*   *   *

The seventies saw the demise of many of the colourful markets, but I was lucky to be able to experience the atmosphere of some of them before they disappeared or moved to new sites around the city.

Although moving them probably made economic sense, it was a shame to see them go. Covent Garden was one favourite of mine and I loved being called down there. It was looking pretty shabby and neglected at that time and its days were numbered, but I would revel in the bustle, confusion and noise. The colours and smells of all the fruit and flowers more than made up for the shabbiness. It was chaotic in the early mornings and trying to find a parking place for the van was a nightmare. Old Minis, Escorts and VW Beetles vied for space with the open backed trucks stacked with crates of produce. Lorries from all over the country and further afield were unloading their colourful cargo. The smells were mouth-watering and almost overpowering. There was rack after rack of juicy oranges and green apples displayed in open boxes in dozens of stalls under a huge glass roof. In fact, there was produce of all types from all parts of the world. The general noise included good-humoured shouting and swearing amongst the drivers and stall-holders. Men valiantly pulled wooden carts through the chaos, stacked high with slatted crates, as though time had stood still. Broken crates, discarded paper and fruit, and flower cuttings were strewn everywhere. Market people were something special and when I turned up on a call, I often became a butt for many of their ribald innuendo and jokes. I enjoyed the odd visit there to collect sick or injured pigeons or cats that lived round the market. The shutters finally came down in 1974 and the site languished for a long time before becoming the tourist area of gift shops, restaurants and museums. When I stand there today watching the street artists, I can still see the market as it had been and the area just does not have the same appeal.

Billingsgate Fish Market was also still operational on the riverside just downstream from the Tower of London. The market was another favourite of mine and I was often called to collect sick or injured seagulls, pigeons and stray cats that were attracted there by the chance of free food. The early morning sight of Tower Bridge from the waterfront on a bright sunny day, far busier with river traffic than now was inspiring. The market reeked. There is no other word for it. The concrete floor was always running with water and fish entrails and you had to be careful where you walked. The porters wore round flat topped leather hats called bobbins which had a gulley round the peak to collect dripping water from the boxes they carried on their heads. They also wore boots and aprons and were always in high spirits. Like Covent Garden, the air was filled with good-humoured shouting and swearing. It was a close knit community and was a fascinating place to wander round. Since ancient times the porters had been licensed and had a job for life. They proudly wore their badges of office and their job was often handed down from one generation to the next. I loved to look at all the weird and wonderful fish on the slabs, but I felt so sorry for them as well. It was fascinating to see the men wielding their knives so deftly as they gutted, trimmed and filleted the fish. Gulls used to hover all-round the market for scraps. They must have been very confused when it closed and became upmarket office space. I wonder if the smell lingers on.

* * *

Many areas of London were historically deprived, with a procession of immigrants passing through. Because of the poverty in these areas, the RSPCA had, over the decades, built up a network of free veterinary clinics. They were located in places like Bethnal Green, Bow, Camberwell, Lee Green, Islington and Edmonton. Over the decades, these clinics did brilliant work in helping tens of thousands of sick or injured animals from these areas of London. Dogs with distemper, cats with flu, dogs with cut paws and broken legs were all attended to for free, or for a small donation. The clinic assistants who manned these outposts were unsung heroes. Most of the clinics disappeared in the early seventies during cutbacks, as it was felt that they were not required as Londoners were not necessarily that impoverished or needy any longer. There are no memorials to these clinics and they are now just a memory to a few.

One of them that survived longer than most was the one situated next door to the Angel Underground Station at 397 City Road, Islington. The clinic had quite a history as its staff had carried out many courageous animal rescues during the Blitz on the East End. The clinic doubled as the training establishment for all staff and it was here that I had undergone my six-month probationary period before becoming a fully-fledged RSPCA clinic assistant. The clinic closed in 1973 and most staff that passed through its doors over the decades had happy memories and nostalgia for the place. I certainly do and I still know many of my contemporaries who have the same feelings.

On the ground floor there was a consulting room and waiting room and on the first floor a small operating theatre. These areas were presided over by 'Miss', the vet and the main character of the establishment at the time. Tall, slim and with long blond hair, 'Miss' cut quite a figure striding out of the Underground Station and up the path to the clinic in her high heels, black stockings, her long raincoat and her black bag swinging from her shoulder. She was one of those people who swept noisily into a room and changed the whole atmosphere. She would plonk herself down in a chair, put a cigarette in an elegant black holder, clamp it in her mouth and demand a coffee. When the clinic was quiet, she had a habit of imitating Marlene Dietrich, both in dress, looks and voice and was not averse to giving impromptu renditions of the song 'falling in love again' complete with accent. She was quite a taskmaster for us trainees and we dreaded quiet spells during surgery times. The surgery was lined with shelves and cupboards packed with rows of jars, boxes containing lotions, potions, and pills. The wonder drugs of today were still in their infancy at that time. Her favourite training ploy was to line all of us up and get us to start at one end of a shelf and name all the drugs and their uses.

'Well John, what is acriflavine used for?' she asked me sitting on her stool and delicately puffing away at her cigarette holder.

I would nervously stare at the shelf trying to remember.

'We went all through this yesterday, didn't we?' she prompted sweetly.

'It's used for burns and scalds Miss,' I tentatively ventured.

'Very good, John. And the next?' she persisted as she plastered more lipstick onto her lips.

And so it went on, while you prayed someone would turn up to have their pet treated and distract her. Although these sessions were dreaded at the time, they really did work, and after a couple of weeks, I knew all the drugs and their uses, knowledge that I have retained throughout my entire career.

'Miss' had an incredible memory and no coffee break passed without her remembering a client she had seen a week or so earlier who hadn't returned as ordered. We would all be sitting in the staffroom collectively completing the Sun crossword, when she would shout 'Mr Stevens hasn't been in with his cat yet. I'm sure he was due back today. Pop upstairs will you Sue and find me his file.'

Sue dutifully ran upstairs, found the card and gave it to Miss who perused it for a few seconds.

'There you are!' she would exclaim with triumph, 'he was in early last week and I told him to come back in ten days. Perhaps he'll be in later.' She sat there puffing her cigarette and contemplating for a few more minutes and then the cry would go up again.

'Mrs Newman should have come in today, I'm sure. Be a darling Gordon and pop upstairs for her card will you.'

Although the RSPCA provided these clinics free to those who could not afford to pay, the clients were expected to make some token donation towards the cost. Many did not and this irritated Miss no end. Her long memory came in useful again, as she would remember a bad payer and do everything possible to extract money from them the next time they came in. There was a glass fronted metal donation box on the surgery table and she would make some excuse to bring it to the attention of the client. Should this fail, she blatantly slid it towards the client often rattling it or slamming it down. Should the client still not heed her tactful persuasion to part with some coins, they would be indelibly imprinted in her memory. The next time

Miss spotted them in the waiting room, she would say: 'that man out there only put a penny in the box last time and I know he could afford more. He thought I didn't see, but I did. Do you remember him John?' she would say to me. Miss would open the surgery door a crack and have me peering through to the waiting room.

'Can you see him John? We'll make sure he pays this time?'

When it was the poor man's turn to enter, she hid the collection box and replaced it with a kidney dish. At the end of the consultation, she stared at the man sweetly and pointed at the dish saying: 'Our donation box is unfortunately broken, but you can put your donation in there instead.'

A two-shilling piece clanged into the dish and she turned triumphantly towards us with a broad smile and a wink. Sadly, it was always those that could ill afford who always automatically paid. This was particularly so with the elderly who felt it a point of honour to at least give something however small. Miss was good at on the spot almoning and when unsure if a client could afford a donation or a private vet, she would delve through the telephone directory. 'If he can afford a telephone, he can afford a private vet' was one of her catchphrases. How times have changed. I wonder on what criteria she would judge people now.

Like most vets, she was not keen on temperamental animals, which threatened to bite or scratch, and it was always the clinic assistant who was the cannon fodder. I hate to think of how many dogs I have grasped in a headlock with the head and jaws tantalisingly close to my face or holding onto a cat's scruff and front legs with determination. Hamsters and Budgerigars were by far the worst for the odd scratch or bite. If the vet received a bite or scratch, it was your fault and if you were bitten through some act by the vet, it was still your fault. It was a daily occupational hazard.

During my second week as a trainee, I vividly remember an incident involving an elderly man who literally dragged his scruffy Pekinese dog into the surgery one morning. The man, wheezing and puffing had neither the strength nor inclination to lift his dog onto the surgery table. Miss immediately volunteered my services: 'Give the poor man a hand to get his dog onto the table will you, John.'

I obliged like a lamb to the slaughter and as I bent low to lift the dog up he latched his tiny jaws onto my nose, which I have to admit is a large target. I cannot adequately describe the pain, but I immediately dropped the dog, which luckily let go and fell to the floor.

'That was a silly thing to do John; you must learn to be more careful,' commented Miss unsympathetically.

I hung my head over the sink pinching my nose and bathing it under cold water in an attempt to stop the bleeding and the onset of bruising. This had little effect and the next morning in the bathroom mirror I was shocked at the sight of the swollen red bulbous appendage in the middle of my face. I just knew it was going to be a nightmare facing my colleagues at work and I was right. Just one look at me resulted in fits of laughter and it took a considerable time before they were in a fit state to start working.

10:

The Final Call

It was one of those sultry London summer afternoons, which are so rare. It was also a Sunday and the streets were packed with scantily clad people with smiles on their faces, busily chatting and generally enjoying themselves. It was mainly for this reason that I had volunteered to take the ambulance down to the West End. Better to be out and about than sitting in our stuffy office. A call had come in regarding a sickly pigeon in a doorway near the bottom of Shaftesbury Avenue, where it joins Piccadilly Circus. My colleague was technically the driver for the shift, but he was quite happy to doze in the chair and answer the telephone if it was to inconveniently ring and disturb him. As he said, it was a long way to go to get a pigeon that probably wouldn't be there when I arrived.

I had another reason for going on the call though. This was my last shift working on the Night Emergency Service. I had been offered an exciting animal welfare job on a faraway tropical island, which had brought out all the David Attenborough traits in me, so I had jumped at the chance, and was to depart in a couple of weeks. I was worried this might be the last time I would be able to attend an incident. It had been an extremely quiet day with few calls as everyone was enjoying the weather rather than worrying about animals in distress. Being out and about had always been my favourite part of the job and I wanted one last memory.

I cruised towards Piccadilly Circus with the windows open, the blowers on and the radio playing. The traffic was quite heavy, but I was in no hurry as the pigeon would probably have been there for hours, if not days, before some kind-hearted passer-by decided to take the time to call us. I just took in the sights and sounds as I waited at virtually every traffic light. However, I was quite relaxed.

When I got close, I searched the buildings for a street number and eventually came to a halt outside the address. It was one of those wide recessed doorways containing two entrances to flats or offices above the shops. I could not see the pigeon from the van, but I could see what looked like a homeless person or tramp curled up in one corner. I got out and walked up to the doorway, and sure enough there was a pigeon slumped in the opposite corner. It was very thin and had a discharge from its nostrils and eyes. It appeared to have laboured breathing as well. It was definitely a very sick bird. During my examination, the homeless person opposite had not stirred and he was curled up in a mixture of clothing, blankets and rubbish even though it was such a hot day. I quietly retreated to the van so as not to disturb him and I grabbed a basket. As I knelt down to retrieve the pigeon I heard movement behind me followed by a rasping high-pitched voice shouting:

''Ere wot you up to then?'

I turned my head and came face to face with what appeared to be the very red and grizzled face of an elderly woman and not the male tramp I had taken the heap of clothing for.

'Wot ya up to?' she shouted again in a definite slurred speech.

Great I thought. This is all I need: an altercation with a drunken female tramp in a busy street. I could see my relaxed and laid-back afternoon being spoilt.

'I'm from the RSPCA and I am here to help this poor old sick pigeon,' I lamely replied.

'Wot for. Nuthin' wrong with him. You leave him alone,' she shouted back.

'I'm afraid he is rather sick and I must take him for treatment,' I stated.

'Who are you?' she enquired again as she fell back on her backside.

'I'm from the RSPCA,' I patiently repeated.

'RSPCA!' she exclaimed, 'you the people who kill all the animals. You murderers. You leave my friend alone. You ain't taking him to kill him.'

She tried to pull herself up from the floor and while she was preoccupied with this endeavour, I quickly placed the pigeon inside the basket and fastened the lid. As I stood up, I felt a hand grab my arm. She had managed to get to her feet, was obviously not finished with me, and was going to continue her defence of her friend.

'You give him back,' she shrilled

'I'm sorry. I cannot leave him here, as he is very sick and will suffer and die. You don't want him to suffer do you?'

'You give him back. 'E's my friend,' she angrily repeated as she tried to grab the basket.

I swung the basket out of her reach and headed for the van dragging the still clutching old woman behind me. We were starting to collect a few puzzled glances from passers-by now, as we were on the roadside in full view of everyone. I tried to open the back doors, but the old woman was becoming belligerent so I gave up, wrenched myself free and dived into the driver's seat. I placed the basket on the passenger seat and quickly locked the doors. I was feeling really pleased with myself until an arm suddenly appeared through the window and grabbed my tie. It was then that I realised that being a hot day, I had left the window open when vacating the van. These were the days before the advent of the clip on tie and soon she was doing a great job of strangling me while continuing to shout 'give me back my friend; you can't take him away from me'. I was beginning to wonder how on earth I was going to extricate myself from the situation. Out of pure panic really, I wound the window up, trapping her arm.

'Please let go or I'll drive off with your arm stuck in the window,' I pathetically shouted at her.

Back came her same response about her friend. I started the engine up hoping this might deter her, but it had no effect. I pleaded with her again and when this was ignored, I decided to take drastic action. With one hand trying to remove her hand I slowly drove off. It had no effect for the first few yards as she just staggered along by the side of the van. I drove slightly faster and eventually her arm disappeared from my throat. I roared off loosening my tie at the same time so that I could breathe again. I could see in my mirrors the poor dazed and unfortunate woman staggering in the road. It was probably not my finest moment as an RSPCA officer, but at the time the only way I could think of ending the situation. To make matters worse I did in fact have to put "her friend" the pigeon to sleep.

As it turned out, it was my last ambulance call, and with reflection, it could not have been a better one to finish on. It seemed in so many ways to embody the whole job for me.

Postscript

I look back at the time described in this book with great nostalgia, as it easily represents the most informative and gratifying period of my thirty year career working with animals, and laid the foundation of fulfilling my childhood dream of spending my life helping animals. For a young lad straight from school and starting out in life, the job was heaven sent and at one point I was so captivated by the work that I couldn't bear to be away from it. Apart from the enjoyment and satisfaction of tangibly aiding the animals, I also met so many wonderful people. It was great that so many members of the public were willing to pitch in and help as in the case of Bert and his crew.

I was also indebted to the London Fire Brigade without whom my work would have been extremely difficult and I would not have been able to rescue so many animals successfully. It was only on the rare occasion that they could not attend and this was usually when they were too busy with a major fire or felt the danger to their men of attempting a rescue was too great. In general, they looked upon animal rescues as a training exercise and a more light-hearted challenge. I tried to call upon their services always as a last resort and looked upon them as the cavalry coming to the rescue. The Metropolitan, River and Transport Police, Underground Staff and many other agencies were also of great assistance and sympathetic to the plight of animals requiring help.

After leaving the Night Emergency Service I never quite recaptured those enlightening and satisfying days, but I went on to experience other adventures working with animals in the UK and abroad. The Service meanwhile carried on its good work for a while, but its days were numbered. Other charities appeared and started to provide similar services, the laws changed and Local Authorities, the Police and the Fire Brigade took on more responsibilities concerning animals. The number of stray and latchkey animals in the city decreased and Veterinary Surgeons provided proper twenty-four hour services. Calls for its assistance diminished and it was gradually scaled down, losing its expertise and identity, until it completely disappeared as a distinct entity in the early eighties. I had been so lucky to experience some of the magic of the original Jermyn Street Night Service and to work for the unit in the last throes of its heyday.

The author awaits the next emergency call c.1972

About the Author

John Brookland worked intermittently for the RSPCA for a total of 18 years in their clinics, hospitals and animal homes. In between, he pursued his passion for combining travel with helping animals, by spending time in Trinidad & Tobago aiding stray dogs, and in the Bahamas as Chief Inspector of the Humane Society in Nassau. Back in the U.K., he was Deputy Manager of the Animal Quarantine Station at Heathrow Airport for 6 years. Having witnessed the cruelty inflicted on animals transported by air, he travelled the world working for a conservation group, researching and documenting the capture and transport of wildlife, which culminated in a campaign to try to improve conditions. He is now semi-retired, lives with his partner in Essex and still tries to travel as much as possible.

If you enjoyed this book, look out for the author's next, due to be published in 2013, which chronicles his exploits battling animal cruelty in the Bahamas.

Made in the USA
Charleston, SC
07 February 2013